D0190742

DROP THE WORRY BALL

HOW TO PARENT IN THE AGE OF ENTITLEMENT

ALEX RUSSELL
TIM FALCONER

Collins

Published by Collins, an imprint of HarperCollins Publishers Ltd.

Originally published by John Wiley & Sons Canada, Ltd.,
in both print and EPUB editions: 2012

First published by Collins in an EPUB edition
and this trade paperback edition: 2014

HarperCollins books may be purchased for educational, business, or sales
promotional use through our Special Markets Department.

HarperCollins Publishers Ltd.
2 Bloor Street East, 20th Floor
Toronto, Ontario, Canada
M4W 1A8

www.harpercollins.ca

Library and Archives Canada Cataloguing in Publication information
Russell, Alex, 1965–
Drop the worry ball : how to parent in the age of entitlement /
Alex Russell, Tim Falconer.

ISBN 978-1-44342-772-2

1. Parent and child. 2. Parental acceptance. 3. Failure
(Psychology) in children. I. Falconer, Tim, 1958– II. Title.

HQ755.8.R88 2012   649'.1   C2011-907376-5

Interior design: Pat Loi

Printed and bound in Canada
DWF 9 8 7 6 5 4 3 2 1

"Full of what is passing in your own head, you do not see the effect you are producing in theirs."

—Jean-Jacques Rousseau,
Émile, or On Education (1762)

Contents

Contents

Contents

Introduction

A mother struggling with her tween daughter consulted the family doctor. He offered a number of suggestions and wrote down some titles of parenting books she could read. As mother and daughter left his office, he tried to be reassuring: "Everything will be fine. Try to stay calm and just take baby steps."

A few days later, the daughter started acting up again, which upset the mother. "Mom! Do what the doctor said," the girl instructed, as Mom slowly lost it once again. "Take baby steps!"

"So what do I do now?" she asked when she came to me.

Good question. But I knew better than to simply give her more advice because, at a certain point, advice does more harm than good. Parenting guides began appearing in the 19th century and helped spur the professionalization of parenting. That led to the great shift away from the long history of tyranny over and abuse of children, although in hindsight we know that not all the rules experts dreamed up were good ones. For half a century many doctors even discouraged mothers from breastfeeding their babies. But, more than that, all the advice has led to the steady erosion of parental confidence and our ability to rely on our own intuition.

After 200 years of guides that have often meant as much grief as help, my goal is to provide a different perspective on your relationship with your children and help you reconsider your ideas about the role of a parent. Simply offering more pointers may just deepen your sense of obligation and your need to get it just right. So this book is not a blueprint for parenting and I've kept the tips, guidelines and commandments to a minimum and concentrated on helping you rethink how you do the most important job any of us will ever take on.

I first started thinking about writing this book five years ago. The idea sprang from my work with children and their parents and with schools. As a clinical psychologist, I deal with a wide range of problems, but over the past decade I've increasingly found myself helping families in the same predicament: children struggling to take on the challenges of school and the big world outside the family home, while increasingly anxious parents and educators work harder and harder to get them on track.

Sometimes these are kids who are "underachieving," putting in a minimum of effort and seemingly unable to appreciate the basics of what people need to do in the world (pay attention to various responsibilities, care about the way we treat others, think ahead). These children and teenagers have a worrying sense of entitlement, as if they have the right to spend their lives in pleasurable pursuits—playing or chilling all day, every day—or at least free from any kind of hardship.

Sometimes experts diagnose children with Attention Deficit Disorder or a learning disability. Identifying these issues can be extremely helpful, but for some families, while the diagnosis sheds light on a child's areas of weakness, it doesn't do anything to solve the pressing problems in the family: Johnny's lack of engagement with school and his parents' increasing frustration with him.

Sometimes the diagnosis refers to emotional problems such as depression or anxiety. Anxiety is on the rise among our children, and when I am not seeing a child who is disengaged from school and achievement, chronically avoiding the stress (anxiety) of school and the big world out there, I am often seeing the opposite: a kid who has entirely bought into the whole competitive, marks-oriented school system we have created, and suffers from anxiety symptoms such as panic attacks, sleep and eating problems, and painfully obsessive behavior. While these children often "achieve" well, their orientation to school and broader reality is troubling: they're able to enjoy their achievement to some extent, but their engagement with the world is not particularly rewarding or even interesting to them. It's about the marks, not the subject matter. By the time they suffer from open anxiety and even panic attacks, their parents' central concern is no longer about school and achievement. It's about their child's unhappiness, and their main goal is now to get her interacting in a more playful and rewarding way with the world around her.

I've found that when parents gain a new perspective on raising children, from infancy on up, they're able to develop relationships with their children that are close and supportive. Under these conditions, children grow up to be young adults who are ready to leave home and thrive in the big world out there. To be successful, parents must avoid getting sucked into today's "over-parenting" culture, and instead provide children with what they actually need: loving support and attention that gives them the confidence and sense of personal responsibility required to take on the world for themselves.

I warn you, though: it's not always easy to play this patient, attentive and non-bossy role. You will have to learn to accept that kids are completely capable of worrying for themselves, that failure is an essential learning experience, and that sometimes it's better to stand back and say little or nothing because watching is often more powerful than acting. Toughest of all may be facing the prospect that once you adopt this new approach, some problems may actually get worse before they get better. But they will get better—they always do if parents successfully become compassionate, interested bystanders who are ready to step in when necessary while safeguarding against the real dangers and catastrophic failures that do children no good at all.

Figuring out how to help those caught up in the Age of Entitlement would not have been possible without the families who have shared their difficulties with me over the past decade. Their stories appear throughout the book, although I have freely altered details, switching genders and races, and often combining elements from different cases into one, in order to get a point across. In fact, the stories in this book come from many places, including my own experiences as both a kid and a parent and those of my friends, as well as from the children and parents I have worked with as a psychologist trying to understand these problems.

Piecing all these stories together was challenging. In May 2010, after several years of working on early drafts of the book, I approached Tim Falconer, an author I play hockey with on Friday afternoons. Like many of my friends, he'd heard the tales of my efforts to write a book while maintaining my caseload. Not a psychologist or even a parent, Tim nevertheless recognized many of the issues I was writing about because they are rampant in our culture and because, as a university instructor, he regularly sees the results of over-parenting. Tim agreed to help me and proved to be a worthy opponent in online Scrabble.

As a kid, I played a different game with my family, a drawing game that always gave us a laugh. We each took a piece of paper folded into three panels and drew a character's head in the top panel—a funny old lady, for example, or a gorilla wearing a beanie with a propeller—and then folded the paper over to conceal the head and extended the neck lines down into the next panel. Then we passed the sheets to the left and drew a body, without knowing what the head looked like, of course. Then we folded the sheet again and passed it along so the next person could add a pair of legs. Finally, the reveal: we unfolded the sheets to look at our creations. Inevitably, there were crazy combinations, such as a gorilla's head on a muscle man's body with two skinny knobby-kneed legs.

Sometimes, writing this book with Tim was a bit like that; we passed it around, adding sections, and having fun. But it's no random creation. The stories in the opening chapters focus on some of the important milestones in children's emotional growth, particularly in the early years, while the later chapters are predominantly about adolescents. If you have older kids, don't skip the first chapters, because understanding the early years will help you understand teenage behavior. And if your kids are younger, now is the perfect time to adopt a new perspective, because even if your children aren't displaying any signs of entitlement, your obligated parenting—and their reaction to it—is setting a pattern that is likely to soon become painfully evident. So drop the worry ball now.

One

Parenting from the Bench

A 5-year-old boy climbs on a jungle gym while his mom sits on the bench with her friend. The boy works away, trying to scramble to the top. Mom knows there are risks—the bars are iron, he is several feet up—but she sits, chats and sips her latte. When the boy reaches the top, he turns and says, "Look at me!" And, of course, Mom does: "Look at you!"

That recognition gives him a sense of accomplishment and pride. Because Mom is present and emotionally available, she can respond to what her son needs from her. By seeing him for "who he is," she confirms his budding awareness of himself and provides him with the confidence that someone is there for him. What appears to be an everyday moment is actually a critical one because that validation and emotional availability are really what our kids most need from us. It is the true heart of parenting. This is how we "mind" our children.

Today's child is the safest in history: streetproofing, bike helmets and fire-retardant pajamas mean a kid really needs to work hard to get seriously hurt. And yet today's parents are the most anxious, guilt-ridden and fearful in history. So, later, outside the playground, Mom will ramp up her involvement in everything her son does. Unlike the playground hazards, the dangers of the real world—poor academic achievement and the possibility of missing out on postsecondary education; drugs and addiction; sex and pregnancy; behavior problems and mental health issues—seem too threatening to sit calmly on the sidelines and enjoy the show. So, too anxious about slipups, many parents get off the bench, worriedly directing their child on the monkey bars of life—advising, guiding, overseeing and often, ultimately, demanding.

The playfulness of the child's exploration slowly wanes under the pressure, and the warm, positive flow that once ran so easily between parent and child fades. Stressed out and frustrated, Mom and Dad don't look anything like they did back in the park: they're certainly no longer sitting on the bench enjoying the show. And the kids? They're no longer saying "Look at me" the way they once did. In fact, they may be increasingly concerned with keeping their activities a secret from their parents.

Hockey Dad

I've been a child psychologist for 15 years and provide assessments and psychotherapy to children and adults, as well as consultation and supervision to schools, teachers and psychologists. But I don't just see struggling parents in my practice: sometimes I am one too. In fact, on occasion I've been only inches away from becoming that crazed hockey dad we're all familiar with.

I stood in the stands of a cold arena watching my then 7-year-old son try out for a competitive hockey team, the same team I'd once played for. It all seemed so familiar: the coaches in green jackets (some on skates, some on the benches with clipboards) and maybe 35 kids on the ice. As I watched intently, hoping to gauge Sam's chances of making the A team, I could see he was clearly in the top 15, probably the top 10. But the Green Jackets, I soon realized, just weren't focused on him. Every time Sam did something—say, dart around a defenseman in a one-on-one drill and fire off a good shot—the coaches weren't even looking.

When they split the kids into two groups, I could see that one consisted of the top 15 or 20 players. And Sam wasn't in it! They'd put him with the B team. "I know what's going on here," I thought, "it's Old Boys' patronage." Sam was new so they weren't going to seriously consider him. The tryouts were a sham.

I marched down to the dressing room. Seeing my smoldering rage, I suppose, a Green Jacket stopped me: "Can I help you with something?"

"What's with Sam in the B group when he's clearly good enough for the A team? Are you guys fairly assessing the kids?" I didn't swear, but I wasn't happy.

I gave him Sam's name and number and Green Jacket said, "Oh, yes, I know your boy," then described him, and his game, accurately: excellent skater, quick and energetic, okay hands, good passer, skates with his head up, a bit on the small side. "Sam's a great little player, and he's going to be even better, but he needs time with the puck, so we're going to put him on defense on the B team where he will quarterback the play and develop over the year. We try to put each child in the best spot for that kid and the B team is the best place for Sam right now."

It was all so reasonable and clear, and I suddenly gained perspective. Sam was in good hands after all. I thanked the coach and retreated—and was really glad I hadn't sworn at him.

Later, I asked myself where and how I had lost perspective. Obviously, I wanted Sam to make this team. Not just any team—I wanted him to be on this team, the Green team. The Green A team. In part, I still like to think, this was about Sam. I knew that he wanted to make the team and that if he didn't, it would be a painful failure for him. So I was rooting for him. But, of course, I'm always rooting for him. What was different this time was how much I wanted it. As if Sam making the team was equivalent to me making the team. This identification with our kids, this lack of separation from them in our minds, can bring out the worst in us.

We all suffer from this a little bit. If you don't believe me, check out a minor league hockey game and see how many parents visibly lose perspective on how much the outcome of the game actually matters, or how unfair the referee is. Often, other than being a rather embarrassing display, this loss of perspective—forgetting that this is their child's life, not theirs—probably doesn't do all that much harm. In fact, to the extent that it brings parents and kids together in a common, enjoyable pursuit, it may do some good. (Watching, and coaching, my kids' hockey teams has given me some of the most exciting sporting moments of my life and they've been great moments in our family's shared life together.) But, as parents, our identification with our children's efforts can quickly lead us away from that all-important "minding" role. Imagine the parent on the park bench who needs his kid to be the next great rock climber and, disappointed with her efforts on the jungle gym, cannot rein in his own feelings: "What are you doing sitting in the dirt? Just do two more climbs. Come on, you can do it!" Seems a bit ludicrous in the playground setting, doesn't it?

At its worst, this loss of perspective can be devastating to a child. I've never been able to forget my minor hockey teammate—the best player on our team—whose father came in after every game and angrily laid into him for all his perceived "mistakes." I can sometimes feel this crazed person inside me when I'm watching Sam. Honestly, when he makes an error (throws the puck up the middle of the ice, say), I feel like he's pushed an old lady down in the mud. "What are you doing?" I want to yell. "Are you insane?"

The crazed hockey dad—and my inner crazed hockey dad—suffers from over-involvement in his children's achievement. He identifies with his kid too much: your win is my win, your loss is my loss. Surely, he'd never act that way in the park, would never yell at his climbing son, "No, not the yellow bars! Take the purple bars!"

Children Once Grew Up; Now We Raise Them

I actually played at the same rink, North Toronto Memorial Arena, where I watched Sam's tryout. The place hasn't changed much over the years, but parenting sure has. After Sam made the team, the coaches called all the parents in for a meeting in the dressing room. As the kids practiced with the trainer on the ice, the coaches passed out binders filled with dietary information, summer workout plans, dress codes and other expectations. As I sat there I thought, "Wow, history's repeating itself." I remembered this dressing room, I remembered the first practice meeting with my coaches back in the 1970s. But back then, the room was filled with eager young players, not anxious parents.

My dad also played hockey at this level at another Toronto arena. He took the bus to all his games and his father never saw him play. Parental involvement in children's lives sure has ramped up since then. Although my parents eagerly supported my hockey, it was rare for both of them to attend the same game, and I wasn't even my dad's favorite player. He loved my buddy Jim Risk, our penalty minute leader. I could always count on hearing Dad's delighted cheer ("Dirty old Risk!") every time Jim took a penalty. My wife, Andrea, and I almost never miss Sam's or our daughter Claire's hockey games—and, on the inside, I'm always cheering loudest for my own kids.

We're involved in our children's lives for lots of reasons but one of the biggest ones is that we're being told to. An example of the social messaging that puts pressure on parents to get involved in their kids' lives came from the *Globe and Mail* on the first day of school in September 2010. At the back of the front section, the paper's editorial board delivered a strongly worded reprimand to "helicopter parents"—the term used to describe our generation of anxious, hovering parents—urging them to back off, even if it meant letting their undergraduate offspring fail. Called "Parents, let them kids alone," it argued: "Left to their own devices, young people may behave badly at university. They may eat too much pizza, drink too much beer. They may have sexual relations in a way that is not in keeping with the mores of their parents. Will they read their expensive textbooks without a parent hovering? Possibly not. But failures such as these, and more serious ones, too, have more uses than many in this generation of parents are prepared to accept. One does not fail if one takes no risks. And one learns little without risk." It concluded: "Parents who wish to create the conditions for success need to stop hovering, and while still being avail able allow their children to take risks, fail and learn from failure. That is how children, and adults, grow."

Great message and I loved reading it in my morning paper. Your kids have to fend for themselves at university. That means you should not go online in the summer to get them into the courses they want to take, show up at their tutorials or contact their professors. If they're going to do a bit of failing in their undergraduate years, fine. That's actually a really good time to find out that they don't live in a childproofed world.

But—and it's a big but—on the same day, in the same paper, the front of the "Life" section featured a full-page article on how to set up your child's study space starting in the third grade. The photo showed an 8-year-old at her desk with the perfect lighting and the article included plenty of information about what kind of lighting to buy, the optimal distance from chair to desk, and the best hours to have the little darling sit down to do her homework. So on one page, the paper demanded that you stop being a helicopter parent, but on another, it told you in no uncertain terms that your child's success was your responsibility. And failure is not an option.

Of course, parents want to meet all the emotional, educational, nutritional and recreational needs of their kids throughout the entire day (and when children do go outside for unstructured play, which happens less and less often, parents are more and more uncomfortable). But the desire to excel at raising kids has led to the "professionalization" of parenting. All the advice, wanted or unwanted, parents receive—from magazines, radio shows, teachers, principals, counselors, doctors, dentists, nosy neighbors and even the dirty looks at the checkout line when a toddler throws an ugly temper tantrum—confirms one message: You are morally obligated to serve your children well. Do not fail them!

And we take that message to heart, doing things for our kids that we have no business doing. One Toronto math teacher decided to offer a weekly tutorial session after seeing his ninth grade students struggle with the curriculum. The first week, half the people who showed up were parents; the second week, most were. Universities now provide special orientation programs for the parents and chiropractors report that their business spikes in September from all that pushing of couches up stairs to dorm rooms. And some parents, the *Globe* reported, are even negotiating employment contracts when university graduates receive their first job offers.

My kids came home from their first day of school with a little book called an "agenda." It's really an espionage log. Their school—like all the others that are part of the Toronto District School Board—expected my wife and me to check Sam's and Claire's homework every day, ensure that it had been completed properly, and sign off on it. Then the kids are to take the agenda back to school the next day to show that their parents are involved in their academic life from day one. The board's intention here is good—research shows that parents who take an active interest in their kids' school lives have children with better school outcomes—but the messaging is way too simple: setting yourself up to be the homework police is not what helps.

We do not want to be in the centre of our kids' academic experience. When children get into trouble in the primary grades, the first thing I have to do is help parents understand that their goal is to help their children develop their own relationship to school and achievement by the time they get to the sixth grade. Parents can't force that relationship to happen. The good news is you don't have to; the mindful, park-bench approach is what works. Pay attention to your children's efforts and experience, be ready to offer support when they ask for it, and recognize what they accomplish. This parenting position puts a child's school experience squarely in his or her own hands, but also sends a message of confidence. By staying on the park bench and giving a child time and space to find his own way, a parent implicitly sends the message: "I believe in you, I know you'll work this out—just give me a call if you need any help."

When parents stand back—interested but not hovering—they send a message of trust that greatly helps their kids take on the challenges of the world. All their anxious hovering sends exactly the opposite message: "We're not sure you have what it takes; this whole school thing is really hard and you're going to need a whole lot of help; without us guiding you through this you'd be lost." Given that message, it's no surprise that more and more children are less engaged in school and what it has to offer, and increasingly intimidated by the challenges of the world.

The irony is that modern, obligated parents who work so hard to nurture emotionally healthy children are actually raising kids who are delayed in their emotional development, kids who increasingly lack the resilience to take on life's problems.

The Island Family and the Family Island

We're parenting our kids in increasingly greater isolation. Once, kids grew up in communities; today, not so much. A typical teenager now spends an average of 14 minutes in unstructured play after school, and there are fewer and fewer kids playing out in the community. Our lives, and even our homes, are designed primarily around our children. That's why kitchen islands— often advertised as the epitome of family togetherness, the ideal place for kids to do their homework while parents cook dinner—are so popular in new and renovated houses.

Although no one planned it this way, today kids live most of their lives inside their family homes or doing family-sanctioned activities. When they're not at home, they're at school (where parents are more involved than ever before), or at an organized sporting or artistic activity (where parents are more involved than ever before). When they play with their friends, they do so on "play dates" organized by parents.

What does the typical day look like? Well, for most of us in urban North American families, it probably looks something like this:

7:30 to 8:15 a.m.
Breakfast: As nutritious as possible, though that often leads to strife and battles, so some parents relent in favor of domestic peace. Make lunches following "get them to eat nutritiously" guidelines from a magazine.

8:15 to 9:00
Deliver everyone everywhere on time. Children are more reliant on parental taxiing than ever before. One reason is greater parental involvement in extracurricular activity; another is increased worry about crime (even though Canada's crime rate is the lowest it's been since 1973, when parents were just fine with letting their kids walk to school on their own, and play in the evening until the streetlights came on).

9:00 a.m. to 5:00 p.m.
Get to work. Try to function.

5:00
Rush home: This is complicated by the need to balance kid pickups, ballet schedules and grocery shopping.

6:00 to 6:30
Prepare dinner while overseeing the kids as they do their homework at the kitchen island.

6:30 to 7:00
Dinner: More battles over the nutritious food prepared with love.

7:00 to 9:00
Monitor "screen time." Check out who the kids are friends with on Facebook.

9:00 to 9:30
Oversee unfinished homework—or, possibly, complete unfinished homework—then bedtime.

10:00
Go to bed.

Next day
Repeat.

It's an exhausting schedule for the adults—but it's really no better for the children to have their parents' fingerprints all over their lives, all the time. There really are fewer and fewer opportunities for kids to do their own thing. Increasingly, our children live in adult-controlled worlds. And it's only getting worse: with the advent of cell phones, for example, we are now tethered to each other 24 hours a day. It's true that with all this time and all these toys, families can have fun together like never before—and do!—but when it's not fun, this can be a crazy-making arrangement.

Childhood Revolution

"Please, Sir, I want some more." Oliver Twist's humble plea and the outraged response say much about what life was like for most children of the Dickensian era. Adults did not suffer the presence of children gladly, and kids, if they knew what was good for them, stayed out of the way.

Until about 250 years ago, adults in the Western world held a kind of tyranny over children. "Better whipped than damned," ran the Puritan saying, and the idea that children should be "seen and not heard," or that they should "speak only when spoken to," was common into the last century. Indeed, for most of recorded human history, the challenges and needs of the young received relatively little attention from the adults living with them. Up until the modern age, the great majority of children were routinely left on their own for much of the day and largely raised by older children when they were "raised" at all. In the Middle Ages, kids were, by today's standards, "neglected," often in ways that proved fatal to them. Medieval children were viewed as small but wayward adults and subjected to a protracted swaddling phase as infants, "leading strings," corporal punishment and general disapproval.

Jean-Jacques Rousseau's observation in 1762 that "childhood has its own way of seeing, thinking and feeling," and his admonition to caregivers to "treat your pupil according to his age," may seem self-evident to us now, but at the time his perspective represented a dramatic shift from the way people viewed children and childcare. Over the 250 years since then, we've gradually come to assume that children have a powerful claim to be understood according to their unique needs, and deserve adult responses appropriate to those needs.

This new attitude has affected the health not only of children but also of the adults they become. Kids can expect to be in the presence of an attentive and emotionally attuned caregiver most, if not all, of the time. As a result, they generally develop the confident expectation that they will be protected and cared for and that someone will be there for them when they need it. These ingredients are the basic requirements for the "secure attachments" we want our kids to develop.

Despite the obvious benefits for children's emotional growth, there have been some troubling side effects. Today, if we don't succeed in producing a "securely attached" child, or one with "good self-esteem," we've failed. So we must have "parenting skills," a concept entirely unique to the modern age. We must be emotionally attuned to our kids, and our responses to their needs must be appropriate for their age. Nothing wrong with that, of course, but it does mean tremendous pressure to do our job correctly—both technically and emotionally—sometimes with negative consequences: overly anxious parents doing too much, out of fear of being neglectful.

If the 18th century marked the beginning of the "professionalization of parenting," with Europe and North America taking an increasingly "scientific" approach to parenting (manuals written by doctors outlined the rules for feeding, bathing, sleeping and toilet training), the publication of Benjamin Spock's *The Common Sense Book of Baby and Child Care* in 1946 marked another turning point in our cultural attitudes toward parenting. Some critics—many of them politically motivated—blamed the book, which has sold more than 50 million copies around the world, for a rise in permissiveness. But Spock insisted he "always advised parents to give their children firm, clear leadership and to ask for cooperation and politeness in return." Whatever else he may have done, Spock launched a massive industry of parenting advice that today includes books, magazines, television shows, websites, blogs and public health campaigns. And yet, most parents are still a long way from getting it right. Many are overwhelmed by all the advice, for one thing, but they're also misunderstanding or misinterpreting what they're reading and hearing.

The problem is, there can be too much of a good thing. If we are unfailing in our efforts to protect and provide, if our children never experience privation and disappointment, they will not develop the ability to deal with these feelings. And accepting them is critical to taking on reality.

Conditioned to understand they're in an adult-operated world, and kept safe by those who control their lives, kids increasingly do what's logical: they learn to please and appease adults when they must, but otherwise avoid them and their world. If the "real world" is that place Mom and Dad always freak out about, who would want to live there anyway? Adult-run reality—school, camps, the job market—means "doing work" and is a place to grudgingly get away with the minimum effort, if you can't stay away from it altogether. Preferring alternative (and largely avoidant) realities such as the Internet, video games, drugs and "chilling" with friends, these kids underachieve academically and sometimes drop out altogether. They often don't know what they're interested in, and if they have any sense of a direction it tends to be vague and unrealistic: "Doesn't matter, as long as I don't have to work too hard, and I make a lot of money."

Boys—teenage boys especially—are most likely to take this avoidant route, but we will meet some girls who've also opted for this solution. There is another response, one typically favored by girls but certainly not exclusively, which is the opposite of avoidance, but no better. This response to adult pressure is to become a pleaser and hoop-jump-through-er. In many ways, of course, this is more adaptive, since the result is pleased teachers and parents; the danger is that the outside world becomes entirely mediated by adult gatekeepers who determine what is right and wrong and what a kid can and can't do. While losing this independent relationship with the outside world may seem a small price to pay, it's not. Children who take this course are not only highly dependent on their parents and teachers, many of these young people become anxious in unhealthy ways. An obsessive focus on marks can lead to crippling perfectionism, highly stress-ful levels of competitiveness with peers, panic attacks, and sudden breakdowns that mean a previously high-achieving student can no longer go to school. These are problems educators increasingly must deal with. At a recent talk at a girls' private school, I heard the principal speaking to the guidance counselor about the number of "cases" they had to deal with the next day. It took me a moment to remember that I was in a school, not a hospital.

Of course, the current generation of young people has many fine traits and much to admire about it. There are many talented, bright and delightful young people. Many of these youth show great tolerance for sexual and ethnic diversity—greater tolerance, in fact, than any generation before them. But all those qualities aside, it's no surprise that this generation, raised by parents who feel obligated to give their kids everything they need, all the time, now feels entitled to everything, all the time.

In my clinical practice, I see cases ranging from autistic children for whom mere communication is a struggle to entitled kids who stole the car keys so they could go out for pizza. More and more, especially in the last six years, the problems I see include a tangle of parents and children that's often full of conflict and always highly stressful. In these family knots, the parents are usually busily and anxiously overseeing the kids' difficulties dealing with the challenges of life, and the children are increasingly falling into one of two positions: the avoidant disengager, or the please-and-appeaser, obsessed with marks and at risk of an anxiety disorder. Younger kids often seem to have too much power in their families, perhaps because the parents' ever-present devotion—the parents' evident need for the children to do well—gives the children unhealthy leverage. Increasingly, those working with children (and, at this point, even young adults) lament a growing lack of respect for parental authority in the home, and not enough engagement with the world outside of it. (I'm not alone in having this view. Recently, I attended a roundtable of psychologists, psychiatrists and social workers. The session was called "What are we treating?" and the discussion focused on kids who are entitled, disengaged and over-reliant on adult support, yet are often defiant and disrespectful.)

I regularly see parents who take their care-giving obligations to lengths that are actually a disservice: the mother who repeatedly provides alternative food choices and is surprised that her daughter is a stubbornly picky eater; the father who made it his mission to help his son with his homework and can't understand why the boy now "doesn't seem to care about school" and expects Dad to deal with the whole business; the mother who, hoping to show how understanding she is, overlooks her son's bad behavior, language and manners and is dismayed that he's oblivious to the consequences of his actions.

Children of desperate-to-help parents can be quite charming and polite, but also tyrannical and controlling, especially with their parents. In my office, these kids often appear defiant, blatantly ignoring or disobeying their parents. This is painful to watch, especially because the parents desperately want to give these kids exactly what they need. They try so hard to get it right and feel so frustrated and guilty about how things turn out. Parents in this predicament often feel one down in the relationship, in a position of servitude. The child is now the master.

What We Worry About

Crazed hockey dads and soccer moms abound, but school and academic achievement trip up more parents than anything else.

They just can't help themselves. They supervise homework, provide reminders about tests, check in with teachers and, more often than not, battle with their children every step of the way. They lie awake at night worrying about report cards, university admissions, careers, The Future . . .

Strikingly, this is exactly what their kids aren't thinking about. The more parents take on these concerns, the more their children are oblivious to them. It's not always clear which comes first—the obligated parent or the disengaged child—but they certainly perpetuate one another. The more a kid turns off school, disregarding his assignments and studying, the more anxious and involved his parents tend to become. The problem is that this makes children even less inclined to engage.

"They're so irritating!" I hear these kids say as soon as the door closes behind their parents. "They're driving me nuts!" For these children, the focus is entirely on their parents and the perceived unfairness of their "nagging." Sometimes, that behavior has been pretty extreme—screaming and yelling, threatening enormous consequences and even splashing water in kids' faces to get them out of bed (a surprisingly frequent action). It's often impossible not to sympathize with the kids.

By their own admission, parents aren't making the world out there seem at all attractive. But it's impossible not to sympathize with them as well. They've done everything for their kids and when that hasn't worked they've tried soft love, tough love and every approach in between. And nothing seems to work. These parents find themselves in a damned-if-you-do-damned-if-you-don't predicament: if they get on their daughter about school, she pushes back and things get worse; if they leave their son to his own devices, he does nothing and it gets worse. No wonder they're anxious.

After academics, the biggest concerns are what I call sex, drugs and video games. Although today's kids are likely the safest to ever walk the planet, it's definitely a scary time for parents. And nothing seems to freak us out more than the digital world, especially with its risks of Internet gaming addictions, Facebook bullying and exposure to violent and sexual material. Teenagers have always explored the world in ways that made their parents uncomfortable. But a generation ago, when teenagers snuck off to the park to learn how to smoke cigarettes, drink warm beer and make out with each other, parents often laughed it off and said, "It's best that we don't know." Today, many people would regard such a statement as immoral or, at the very least, incorrect.

But here, just as it does in the area of academics, parents' efforts to guide and protect their children can easily backfire. Anxious about their child's whereabouts, distrustful of his friends or suspicious about her activities, parents become inquisitive. "Where are you going after school?" "Who's going to be at the party?" "What's in your backpack?" More often than not, such questions do more harm than good—teaching the child to keep a low profile, and to tell parents what they want to hear.

Again, it's almost always impossible to know which came first, the evasive kid or the intrusive parent, but parents lament to me: "We don't know what she's thinking anymore." Or: "We can't trust him anymore; he never gives us the full story." Efforts to investigate things more thoroughly just make kids more careful and guarded. It's a tough spot for parents: Ask questions and investigate and it seems to further alienate your child; ask nothing and feel like you don't know who your child is anymore.

One of the trickiest parts of parenting is learning how to guide and protect your children yet leave them to their own devices enough that they develop their own ways of coping with the big, bad world. We have to do both. We must be active in our children's lives, at various times teaching them directly, controlling their freedoms, or advocating for them. At the same time, we need to do the opposite: we need to be park-bench sitters in our children's lives: interested and available, but relatively inactive, giving them their freedom and letting them learn on their own, making mistakes along the way. Fortunately, we don't need to be perfect parents (perish the thought!), just good enough. But if we're going to make mistakes, we need to err on both sides of the line. And this means we need sometimes to err on the side of neglect.

This is true even for kids with special needs. One of our great advances in child development is how much better we are at identifying children's areas of weakness and vulnerability. The great example is attention and distractibility problems. Where once these children would have been marginalized in the classroom and their lack of conformity labeled as misbehavior, we can now identify them and help teachers develop an educational plan for them. It would be impossible to overstate the value of this kind of accommodation: among other things, where students are already at a disadvantage in the classroom, they no longer need to add a sense of being "dumb" or "bad" (or often both) to the challenges they already face.

Children with Attention Deficit Hyperactivity Disorder (ADHD) require a little more guidance and advocacy than others. Not to step in as a parent and provide extra support to a child like this, particularly in the early years, would be a great disservice. Still, the balancing act remains. It's all too easy to take on too much responsibility and push your child into a pattern of learned helplessness. That's when it becomes unclear how much of a student's school problems are because of what he can't do, and how much are because of what he simply isn't doing (because he's ignoring it or avoiding it or "doesn't care"). And suddenly we're back on familiar turf: faced with a seemingly disengaged child struggling in school, the temptation for parents is to become more active in the child's life, which just increases the alienation.

As with any other kid, the child with learning challenges has to develop her own relationship with school and achievement. So the parents must straddle the line between assisting and guiding (enough to protect her from too much frustration and failure) and sitting back enough to send the message that school is her business, that the parent is just there to lend a hand when necessary.

The Worry Ball

Let me assure you of one thing: children are not missing the part of their brain that allows them to become anxious for themselves. And yet, much of my work involves convincing parents to put down "the worry ball" so their kids can pick it up. Think about the mom in the playground who is too anxious to stay on the park bench. She busily spots her son on the jungle gym, perhaps warning him not to go too high. Parents who do this—and I've heard more than a few confess to it—lose an opportunity to not only take part in their child's exploration of the world, but to foster his or her emotional growth and independence.

Like over-identification, anxiety can distort our perspective and interfere with our developing relationship with our children. Of course, as parents we have to choose safe parks—literally and metaphorically. But once we have our kids in schools, sports leagues and summer camps we deem safe, our kids do best when we return to the bench. We should aim to be emotionally present, interested and ready to help, but let them make choices about what to do on the monkey bars so that when they fall and it hurts, they can become anxious about it—instead of relying on us to do it for them.

The trap for so many parents, who continually act on their anxiety by directing, organizing, prohibiting and reprimanding, is that they take on this role for their child—become "the custodian of reality"—giving implicit permission for the child to continue ignoring reality (since Mom and Dad clearly have that base covered). After all, it's no fun being anxious and, frankly, reality can be a drag, so it's much easier to let Mom and Dad do the worrying and focus instead on appeasing them (and then going back to "chilling" and having fun).

As long as Mom and Dad are happy, everything's good—this is the "first world," the one we begin our lives in. But, like it or not, we need our children to leave this first world and enter "reality" (or the "second world") and that involves taking on anxiety for themselves.

Unfortunately, kids won't pick up that worry ball unless and until parents put it down. And, as we will see with the families you'll meet in this book, the transition means the situation invariably gets worse before it gets better. Parents struggle with the task of putting the worry ball down—often long after they've accepted the basic logic of the idea. Once parents manage to put it down, and children realize they have to pick it up, the children will do almost anything to avoid the inevitable and get their parents to pick up the worry ball again. They may go out of their way to trumpet their nonchalance about the difficulties in front of them. In one family, where the mom worked in her son's high school, the boy continued to sleep in and miss class after the parents stepped back, but after a few days he began to loiter about in the hallway outside his mom's office, right in her line of vision. "I'm your problem," his actions seemed to say. When I suggested she close her door, he actually came in and began bugging and poking her, as bored little boys do the world over.

"Smell their fear," I say to the parents encouragingly. And as odd as it may seem, a little bit of fear on the part of the kids is exactly what I want those parents to aim for.

Painful, Non-Catastrophic Failure

Obviously, we don't want our children to get expelled from school, become drug addicts, fall into crime, get pregnant or contract a sexually transmitted disease. Catastrophic mistakes aren't helpful. But non-catastrophic ones sure are. In fact, making mistakes is absolutely central to the learning process. When our kids make a non-catastrophic error in the world—she blows off a math test, say, or goes out with her friends instead of studying—parents must force themselves back to that park bench. If she hasn't studied, she may well fail; and if she does, it will hurt. It really will.

When it hurts, she learns. It's as simple as that. The only thing that can interfere with it is parental meddling. So though we obviously don't want our kids to know it, we should actually cheer for non-catastrophic, painful failure.

We get this right when she's 4 years old. No parents want their child to get to age 10 and never have had a skinned knee or a scraped shin. Such physical bumps and bruises are the stuff of life and we know intuitively that they're good for our children. As a result, when mishaps in the playground occur—a child is running around, trips and falls and scrapes her knee—we don't remonstrate and review how it must be done next time: "You've got to pick up your feet more and look where you're going! Here's how you run!" No, we just say, "Oh, that's too bad," give her a pat on the back and send her back out to play in that wild, crazy world.

In fact, if anything, we are likely to downplay the consequences, knowing that doing so helps a kid ignore the pain and keep playing. At this age, we know that subjecting children to these little injuries and downplaying their significance builds resiliency. So we normalize and downplay "mistakes."

Yet, parents find this remarkably hard once their child leaves the real playground and enters the metaphorical playgrounds of school and other "real-world" places where a child must deal with external authority figures—neighborhoods and shopping malls, for example. Suddenly, in these contexts, a child's mistakes take on a whole new meaning, leading parents to forget that they made many of these same "mistakes" when they were young. These days, it seems almost impossible for parents to refrain from involving themselves in their children's mistakes: reprimanding, demanding explanations, requiring plans for avoiding this in the future, reviewing possible next steps, lessons learned or—and perhaps this is the granddaddy of them all—sharing with them a story from your own childhood in which you overcame terrible hardships with great resiliency.

I call this finger-wagging. The fact that it never helps doesn't stop parents from doing it. Even "reviewing" a bad outcome dispassionately with a child can convey an unhealthy level of parental pressure. A parent who finger-wags—who says, "See what happens when you don't study!"—does only one thing: takes the child's attention off the real world where her mistake has consequences and brings it back on the (now-resented) parent. The opportunity for learning has been lost.

Children respond in one of two ways when parents require them to meet their obligations out there in the world: passively do what they are told (the bare minimum allowed under the system) or defy the controls and not do what we demand of them. Neither is a good outcome.

Finger-wagging invites both their attention and their resentment—neither of which we want in this moment. Worse, when you do everything for a kid and fret about whether she'll get it done, it certainly doesn't contribute to her confidence. When, instead, we sit back and relax, when we don't freak out about their errors, we send a comforting and encouraging message to our kids that gives them confidence that they're going to make their way in the world. That's why, when our kids do mess up, our response should be, "Ouch! That must have hurt. Can I make you some soup?" Or some version thereof. When we respond with "Ouch!" we send the message that it's normal to make mistakes. That's a message of confidence and the implication is, "I totally trust you and believe you're going to make it someday."

The Park Bench

My friend Lisa has three kids and sometimes juggling all their activities can be a challenge. One day she told her son, who was in the tenth grade, "Ben, I can't pick you up after your game tonight. You'll have to take the bus home."

He was fine with that. "Okay," he said. "I know the way."

She gave him money for his Gatorade and the bus. Alas, doing the right thing for your kids isn't always easy. Ben bought his post-game drink, then waited at the bus stop—until another mom saw Ben standing there and was horrified. She pulled over and picked him up and then called Lisa to say, "Do you know what's happening here? Ben is standing on the street waiting for the bus! Don't worry, I've got him in my car. I'm taking him home."

This kid was 15 years old, would soon be learning how to drive a car and was just three years away from university. Taking a bus should have been something he didn't think twice about, should have been a regular form of transportation for him—and something that certainly shouldn't have alarmed other parents. But there is so much pressure on us to give our kids what they need all the time that it's easy to forget they don't always need us.

That's why I encourage parents to err on the side of benign neglect. Think about how your parents raised you. How much more freedom did you have than you give your children? Think of the mistakes you made and what you learned from them. We don't need to be available to our kids all the time, especially as they get older. Even when our kids are young we want them to fall down and scrape their knees from time to time; we don't want to protect them in bubble wrap. As they get older and have more capacity, we want to increasingly step back, letting go of our active, overseeing role so they learn to cope on their own.

The *Globe* editorial got it right, though: Don't hover around your kid all the time. Once you've checked out the park, and determined there are no syringes in the sand—part of your parenting duty is to make sure your child is in a safe community—it's time to sit on the bench. Not absent, but not over-involved. Pay attention to what she's doing, ready to get involved if she asks for your help or an encouraging "Look at you." Maybe it's just recognition, maybe it's something more substantial: "Mom, can you help me with my homework tonight?" Since that's very different than making her do her homework, you can say, "Yes, of course, I can. I've got 20 minutes between now and when I have to make dinner, will that do?" You don't have to turn your whole evening over to her, just be available. Don't let your anxiety fire you up so that you're off that bench showing yourself and the world what a good parent you are. Just sit on the bench and sip your latte.

This will be hard to do and sometimes you will feel like a bad parent. But you will be doing the right thing for your kids and ensuring they succeed on the jungle gym of life.

Best of all, when you do a good enough job as a bench-sitting parent, you actually get to truly enjoy the show. I learned this, painfully, watching my kids play hockey, needing to get in there and teach, coach and direct. After a loss, I needed to know what the coaches said. Did they review Sam's egregious giveaway in the second period? His stupid penalty? My need to know inevitably led me to ask, nonchalantly as it were, "So, Sam, what did the coaches say?" Sam's answers were never what you'd call forthcoming. Minimalist, in fact. "Nothing" and "I don't know, I couldn't hear" were two of my favorites.

To turn this around, I had to really rein in my own agenda, which had become impossible to conceal. Nothing would do but complete denial of my own need to know. This meant suppressing the urge to ask questions. All questions. Once I did, Sam soon filled the car rides with his own topics of conversation: cool things he had seen on the Internet; strange, surprising questions about things I'd never thought about ("Do moons have moons? *Can* moons have moons?"), sensational assertions of fact of dubious validity. Entertaining though.

Our car rides became fun again. Eventually, I proved myself enough, became enough of a true bench-sitter, that hockey became one of his topics again. (Never, though, on the subjects that I really wanted to talk about: what I thought best for the team and for Sam as a player. And I had sooooo much to contribute!)

"Dad, did you see when we killed that two-men-down penalty in the third?"

"Yeah!" I had: Sam had taken himself out of position going for a big hit, leading to a golden scoring chance for the other team that went off the post. Did I dare to hope that he wished to reflect upon his goonish ways? Alas, no.

"Did you see me cream that guy?" he asked excitedly.

Ah, alas indeed. This is what we get. Still, it is good. These are the tiny and irreplaceable pieces of a child's unique personality and history. And our presence is essential to make them real. In the end, they are at the heart of all that matters.

Two

Obligated Parents
and Entitled Kids

Matt caused his parents no end of grief. The strong-willed 8-year-old refused to go on family outings—or, if he did go, he refused to get back in the car to return home. His constant "push back" meant Cameron and Beth found themselves in what seemed like a never-ending battle to get their son to follow the rules and expectations of the house. Matt also frequently fought with his younger brother, 5-year-old Colin, and while they could both be instigators, it was usually Matt, either by being stubborn and unreasonable or being deliberately provocative. Both parents found themselves doing way too much refereeing and, despite their efforts, they didn't feel as though they were getting anywhere. In fact, things were actually getting worse.

Matt regularly dragged out routine tasks such as brushing his teeth, turning off the TV, getting dressed, putting his coat on—when he did them at all. If Cameron and Beth pushed, Matt just became more obstinate, and the situation escalated quickly. So, although they knew it was bad to give in, they sometimes did. They could stay on 24-hour alert, always preparing for the next battle, or decide it just wasn't worth it to keep battling. Because they were always aware of Matt's readiness to lose his temper or be openly defiant, they found themselves constantly "tiptoeing on eggshells," as they put it—organizing the family in ways designed to avoid Matt's protests and challenges. But the more they tiptoed, the more they had to tiptoe, since Matt was confirmed in his belief that he was entitled to exactly what he wanted. By the time they came to see me, they realized their son ran the show in their house—and he was doing it with the tactics of a terrorist.

Meanwhile, at school, the third grader had started landing in trouble on a daily basis. He was defiant, and was engaging less and less with his peers and with the program. When Matt decided the class "Business Day" wasn't for him, he refused to be a part of it—wouldn't contribute to his group's project. His school, an alternative school, stressed working with kids' strengths and finding a way to accommodate their difficulties, so the staff "worked" (read: negotiated) with Matt and found him a role he'd accept. As business manager, he oversaw the entire grade's projects, and didn't have to contribute to his group's initiative at all. He had no responsibilities beyond bossing everyone else around. But even this solution collapsed the day Matt learned another student would share the role with him.

Cameron and Beth contacted me on the advice of their family doctor. At our first meeting, they began by asking if they had been doing some "bad parenting." They wondered if they'd been too "democratic," offering their son too many choices, providing too many explanations. After talking about this for a few minutes, and reflecting on Matt's argumentative, uncooperative and, at times, belligerent nature, Cameron mused, "Have we created a . . . ?"

His unfinished sentence said so much about the couple: their awareness that they were playing into and even fostering the problem; their frank, thoughtful approach to the situation; and their reflexive reluctance to say anything as negative as "monster" (even though Matt wasn't in the room). There is a certain irony to Cameron and Beth's concern that they were engaged in "bad parenting," since here were two people who had clearly put all their energy, hearts and minds into the job. If there was "bad parenting" here it was a result of them trying too hard to be good parents, being too patient, too reasonable, too available and too accommodating.

I call Cameron and Beth and others like them "obligated parents" because of how deeply and, in fact, how unthinkingly they accept responsibility for their children's healthy development. Taken individually, each one of their actions and reactions makes sense—it's good to be patient with your child, good to be reasonable and accommodating. Taken together, though, these unceasing efforts to support, redirect and organize Matt backfired because they unwittingly sent the message that he was always entitled to this support and accommodation. They were also telling him that he was: a) not required to take things on for himself, and b) not required to accept anything he didn't really like.

Obligated, over-involved parents tend to raise entitled, disengaged kids. It's an epidemic, with cases ranging from mild to extreme. The more disengaged or inappropriate a child is, the more active and involved parents tend to become. But as Beth and Cameron found out, the more active and involved parents get, the less engaged and responsible children behave.

Matt was constantly forgetting to take important things to school—homework assignments, permission forms, gym clothes, you name it. So Beth and Cameron felt obligated to keep track of what he required, reminding him, re-reminding him and then, often, just taking it themselves. But, of course, the more they worked at this, the less Matt had to. Once this vicious cycle starts, it is awfully hard to stop. Because Matt appeared utterly clueless about his responsibilities at school, his parents monitored them closely and badgered him about what he needed to do. Because his parents were constantly badgering him about school responsibilities, Matt increasingly tuned them out, becoming ever more clueless about what he should be doing.

Cameron and Beth also engaged him in long, stressful arguments whenever he refused to accept something not to his liking. He was a gifted arguer, they admitted, a great splitter of hairs and adept at raising technical issues. They described him as a "legislator" with his endless efforts to organize things to his liking—ironic, given his defiant, lawless ways. But because his parents felt obligated to offer reasonable explanations for their decisions, Matt felt he was always entitled to them. And because he felt entitled to a complete and satisfying explanation, and argued and protested until he got it, his parents felt ever more obligated to satisfy him. It's true that it's good for kids to have reasonable and respectful parents who feel children deserve some explanation as to why they've organized things as they have—parents who don't wish to be dictators, that is. But at times Cameron and Beth needed to refuse to dignify Matt's behavior with a response. Their willingness to engage him, no matter how ridiculous his attitude or idea, sent the unfortunate message that such ridiculousness was still allowable, and in this sense, it encouraged Matt to go there again in the future.

As we talked about these vicious cycles, Cameron laughed, recalling the "discussion" he'd had that morning. Late for school drop-off as usual because Matt was dragging his heels and being a pain, Cameron managed to get the boys to the car and opened the trunk to grab two juice boxes. His hands full, he asked Matt to get the juice boxes, but Matt predictably refused. What ensued was increasingly exasperating for Cameron as he attempted to point out that Matt would want that juice come lunchtime, that it was not unreasonable for a parent to ask a child to pick up a couple of juice boxes, that this debate was making them later and so on. All of this as they stood by the trunk of the car in front of the neighbors. Matt refused to get his drink because it "wasn't fair" (Colin didn't have to get his), and Cameron, feeling he couldn't let the boy go to school drink-less, but not wanting to "give in" and get it for him, felt he had no choice but to continue the "discussion."

He shook his head: What in the world had kept him in such an absurd discussion? Why didn't he just say, "Fine, go without your drink then" and move on? These, of course, are the good questions that occur once parents start to gain perspective on their obligated parenting and its unfortunate results.

The Age of Entitlement

Conversations about "kids these days" invariably feature some of the same observations: they sure text a lot, they have extraordinary interest in online diversions, we devote an immense amount of programming and resources to them and, just about always, a reflection that they have such a sense of entitlement.

Entitlement is a belief that I am deserving of certain privileges, a sense of deserving what I get. This attitude stands in opposition to a sense of appreciation: if I feel entitled to what I'm given, I won't feel particularly appreciative of it. It's simply what I'm due.

But it's more than that. When folks use this word to describe their kids—or, even more often, someone else's kids—they're also identifying an attitude toward life in general. Entitled kids seem oblivious to the actual cost of things and to their own good fortune compared to the rest of the world. They take for granted what their parents give them and seem clued out when it comes to appreciating the actual value of things. In an important sense, they are out of touch with the real world.

Seventeen-year-old Sarah, for example, expected her mom to rent a cottage for her and some friends. She told me with a soft smile: "I don't want to sound rude, but we don't really want our parents around." And this was a kid who had failed a high-school course the semester before and had no summer job. She and her friends enjoyed a number of activities together, but drinking vodka was currently one of their favorites. Her idea—completely unrealistic—was that Mom would rent them a place to drink to their heart's content for a week. When I asked her if she thought any owners would want to rent their cottage to a group of teenagers, she said, "Well, yeah, okay, maybe 'she,'"—referring to her mother—"could come for a day or two." The implication, I guess, was that Mom would fool the owners into believing she'd be there the whole time.

When her parents stopped coughing up money without strings attached, and tied an allowance to the successful completion of her around-the-house responsibilities first, Sarah complained. She really believed her mom was "being mean," and "intentionally making things hard on me" by not financially supporting her trips to the mall and other plans, such as the March Break trip to the Caribbean, an unchaperoned high-school pilgrimage that had become a "tradition" (and therefore, in Sarah's mind, a rite of passage, and so, an entitlement). Her reaction to not getting her way was shock and outrage—a genuine sense of being treated unfairly.

To the extent that they feel entitled, kids simply expect things. They feel deserving (regardless of their own conduct), failing to appreciate what they do have and feeling enraged by what they can't have. When they don't get those things, they complain, often loudly. That's when the teenager's rage doesn't seem that different from the 2-year-old's tantrum. And it isn't. As with the 2-year-old, it represents a refusal to accept the limits of reality.

But how much cruel reality do any of us really have to put up with these days? At least those of us living in the developed world, a world of unprecedented comfort, convenience and self-indulgence? We live in the Age of Entitlement: our daily lives are far removed from the necessities of animal existence. Today we feel entitled to so many daily comforts that were once considered luxuries. So when the power goes out or garbage workers strike or gridlock makes driving a frustration, we are incensed: "I have a right to [electricity, garbage removal, get to work]!" We insist our technology always work and our machines always run smoothly and completely safely—and if anything goes wrong, it's the manufacturer's fault.

Meanwhile, we expect doctors to cure every ailment, heal every injury and replace every wonky joint. Even death is an affront to us, accustomed as we are to having things prevented and then treated when they can't be prevented. We are outraged when someone young—certainly anyone younger than 60—dies. All human beings once lived in the constant presence of death, and saw it as a part of life, but it is almost a stranger in our society. We feel entitled to life.

There is a hidden assumption in our attitudes toward death, physical risk and the possibility of getting hurt: if a potential injury can be avoided, it must be avoided. Left unchecked, this idea can have some absurd results. In the late 1990s, city officials removed dozens of school playgrounds in Toronto due to safety concerns. Ours was one. It was a large, rambling structure made of old railway ties, with tire swings and a long plastic tube for a slide. Our children played there practically every day and we were astonished when an earnest safety inspector showed up and indentified for us all the horribly unsafe elements we had been exposing our children to. The tire swing, it turned out, was a "choking hazard," the two-foot perimeter retaining wall was a "tripping hazard." The entire structure was gone the following week.

It's not just that people make such ludicrous decisions in our safety-mad and often insurance-driven society. It's the sanitizing effect this attitude has on childhood and child development. Do we really want our kids to reach adulthood without ever facing any risks or ever having had to fend for themselves? Probably not. But if we're going to stop the madness, we are going to have to make the decision, at times, to place safety second, to say, "Even though this could cause some pain and suffering we're going to allow it to happen." But this will mean taking a stand against the current powerful wave of entitlement—entitlement to life, entitlement to health and entitlement to complete safety.

Getting Perspective

Our parental actions and reactions, and in fact the way we understand our role as "parents," is powerfully influenced by our historical context. We can easily mistake this context for simply "the way things are." But, as I said in the previous chapter, our Western notion of parenting skills is less than 250 years old and for the entire stretch of human history before that, things were the other way around: children felt obligated to their parents, and parents felt entitled to their children's obedience and service.

Almost all parents I see—professionally or socially—acknowledge that on some level they "over-parent." While not all of us are full-blown helicopter parents, almost all of us are at least "helicopter-lite." Despite knowing this, doing things differently and not falling into the current trend is exceedingly difficult. Gaining historical perspective helps us see that we can get off the merry-go-round. It helps to know that we are making our parenting "choices" within the context of a particular historical moment, caught up in a trend that is bigger than we are. In other words, if we're over-parenting, it's not our fault, at least not entirely. But we can stop doing it—if we're willing to step out of the cultural mainstream and take a different route.

The sense of entitlement that defines us now is an attitude, a basic belief in individual rights and privileges that is the fruition of a cultural shift, more or less 250 years old, toward a secular, rational and individual-based society. It's the same cultural shift that brought "children's rights" into public discussion. In this sense, our Age of Entitlement is the logical and perhaps inevitable outcome of the changes that began in the 18th century, with the Age of Enlightenment.

Also known as the Age of Reason, the Enlightenment was an intellectual coming-of-age in Western societies. It led to the French and American revolutions, and therefore to modern democracy, and it's the genesis of "the American Dream." It was also the beginning of modern science and medicine; and it is the age in which Rousseau wrote his famous work on child development, ushering in a new era for the child, with the first child-protection societies, and the first doctor-prescribed childrearing directives.

The notion of inalienable human rights is central to this intellectual development. Human rights became the highest value, higher than religion or the might of hereditary kings. After the Enlightenment, we moved toward a society in which every person has the right to make something of himself or herself—this is the individualism in the American Dream. As the notion of individual rights took center stage, ideas of moral-ity—what is not just right and wrong, but what is good and bad—became less tied to religion and more to the relativistic position that what's good is what's in a person's best inter-est. Today, many people's basic moral stance is that they have the right to make their own choices "as long as it doesn't hurt anyone else."

With the gradual fading of religion as the organizing moral center of our culture, the family and the protection of children has taken its place. It's as if the family is the holy object of our society—anything that is good for the family is good; any-thing that is bad for the family is bad (in a moral sense, at least). Upholding the rights of the middle-class family has become a core value everyone—including the media and politicians—can subscribe to. The family unit is our most sacred entity: adults centered around the child, fulfilling their hallowed duty. In the past, if a kid was unruly or off track it was attributed to the "devil" within: children were "born that way," according to the concept of original sin. Today, when a child is unruly, we blame the parent. And there is definitely a moral quality to our judgments about good and bad parenting. Certainly, it is hard to think of anything that arouses our indignation more than the exploitation or abuse of children.

My experience is that parents feel under a moral obligation not to fail their children. This carries with it both a terrible dread related to the thought of being a bad parent, and the moral supe-riority of carrying out society's apparently highest task. "Baby on Board!" shouts the dangling little sign in the back of the new parents' car window. At the same time, we're buying into today's cult of domesticity, which is the contemporary expression of the American Dream and the cult of the individual. We invest tremendous energy in our own homes and families, prettifying them at home improvement stores, and bettering our children at "child improvement stores," the 7-Elevens of after-school tutoring that now proliferate. And society tells us this is good.

Protecting and raising the young is the most, and perhaps only, sacred function in our increasingly secular culture. So pity the parents who buy into it all and seem to excel at the responsibility, only to get an angry, defiant child. His school isn't getting anywhere with him and, in fact, seems to be turning to the parents for the solution (or is it blaming the parents?). It's not hard to see how these parents come to feel that they're not getting what they're entitled to. Given all we've done for our kids, many of us, if we're honest, probably feel that we're entitled, at the very least, to an educated, law-abiding and reasonably respectful young adult at the end of it.

No wonder I often see people fume over their children's failures. These parents believe they deserve so much better. This is particularly true with high achievers; after all, they've succeeded in every other area that mattered—stayed on top of things, anticipated problems, come up with solutions, acted responsibly, were prompt—so what's the problem here? You can almost feel them shaking their fists at the heavens. "I don't think this is too much to ask!" they complain, practically challenging me to explain how this could have happened.

Sometimes parents will turn this sense of entitlement toward their children's schools and sports teams. School administrators tell me the attitude they often see is: "We paid for it (the education) so we should get exactly what we want"—whether that means no detention, an extension on an assignment, or whatever. And if I'm honest, I have to admit that I've "acted entitled" myself. When I accosted the hockey coach demanding an explanation of what was happening at the tryout, I clearly felt entitled to my son's success.

Whose Problem Is It?

Cameron and Beth didn't arrive at their predicament alone. As the school's response to Matt's stubbornness suggests, it was operating under the same sense of obligation to accommodate and support the boy at all costs. So he was learning the same thing at home and at school: if you don't like it, you don't have to do it. Over the past decade or two, educators, driven by the best of intentions, have increasingly taken on the role of supporting and accommodating students who struggle. Left unchecked, though, this "no student fails" approach has led to unfortunate consequences.

A vice-principal at a publicly funded high school in Toronto where I was consulting on these issues sent me this e-mail: "It seems that teachers are being overwhelmed with forms, workshops, new initiatives and new pedagogy with the intent of trying to make them more accountable for their failures. The more teachers do, the less that students have to do. It seems that we are constantly 'dumbing down' the curriculum in the name of 'student success' with the result that education is no longer a challenge to most students. We have multiple intervention programs designed to increase the accumulation of student credits. Yet it appears at least here that the results have been less than favorable, given the escalating absentee rates and poor recovery credits. The question then becomes where are we going wrong? Or is this symptomatic of the entire education system?"

In fact, it's symptomatic of our education system and of our obligated approach to childrearing more generally. Too often these days teachers and parents are working harder than the students, something that can create a good deal of tension among all parties. When both teachers and parents are under such a powerful obligation to produce developmental success at every step, it is often only a matter of time before they start blaming each other in the event of child failure. To mix metaphors, teachers and parents are playing hot potato with the worry ball, while the avoidant kids are off doing their own thing, oblivious to all the adult struggles. Nowhere is this more evident than when it comes to parent–teacher interviews, an event dreaded equally by both sides, for the same reason: the expectation of being blamed and judged negatively.

A heartbreaking tale I heard from an immigrant parent throws this issue into relief. Just recently settled in Canada and struggling with the language and economic hardship, Fadi and Anjali had to work long hours to survive financially. When they began to receive notes from their son's fifth-grade teacher regarding unfinished homework, given their long work hours, the parents struggled to bring him to task. As the tone of the teacher's notes became more urgent and demanding—remember the teacher was under tremendous pressure to not let the child fail—the parents became increasingly anxious. Finally, in desperation, Anjali took action: she spanked her child and then told him to tell the teacher that she had done so—at least the teacher would know she was doing her duty. Sadly, and perhaps predictably, her strategy backfired: the teacher notified the Children's Aid Society.

Fadi and Anjali's story had a happy ending, though. The school had the resources to step in and help the parents support their son. But this case is an illustration of how, when adults assume this level of responsibility for children, and work this hard to direct and protect them, it can throw the adults into conflict and interfere with children's developing ability to take care of themselves. It's no surprise that developing "resiliency" is the hot research topic among educators. Over the past decade, kids raised in this climate of overprotection have become less and less able to cope with the demands of life and to persevere, and thus a research industry was born.

But given that a lack of resiliency may be the result of too many resources and accommodations in the first place, pouring more resources into these kids to help them with a problem such as resiliency is a self-defeating enterprise. Matt's inability to cope with the demands of his school's Business Day are a great example of this. A critical component of resiliency is a tolerance for frustration, something that was clearly in short supply in his case. In order to grow up, stick with things and take on the world effectively, Matt needed to develop a greater capacity to withstand frustration and disappointment. But he'd received so much "support" that he'd never really been forced to deal with harsh realities.

Kids develop resiliency because they have to.

The easy solution would be a return to the old days when strict parents had the "upper hand" and obedient children submitted to their adult masters. But that would be a mistake. Our modern understanding of the emotional needs of children is significant progress. By being attuned and responsive to their needs, we help kids feel secure, and no sensible person would suggest bringing back old forms of oppression such as strapping, scolding and emotional domination. But we do need to find a balance that gives children what they need without allowing our sense of obligation to drive us into being so attentive, so afraid of failing them, that they feel entitled to this unfailing response.

Minding versus Acting

I met Matt just once. His parents brought him to a session at my request, though they felt certain he'd be resistant and were clearly nervous about the inevitable confrontation. They managed to coax him into the building and up the elevator but he refused to come into my office. He even ignored my greeting. I told Cameron and Beth we'd start anyway and when we went into my office, I left the door open. Matt stayed in the waiting area, about 30 feet away but out of sight.

Beth fretted about this. She wanted to make sure that "something got done" during our hour and was eager to get on with it. I reassured her that we were getting on with it, and eventually she and Cameron became engaged in our discussion. That's when Matt switched from moping in the hallway to sneaking closer to us. At one point, he even moved the potted plant and hid behind it as if he were Wile E. Coyote lying in wait for the Road Runner behind a cactus.

As we kept up with our talking, the plant moved closer and closer until we pulled out some spongy balls and started to bomb the plant. The plant bombed us back and, before long, Matt joined us in the room. Both parents—but Beth in particular—were eager to ask him questions, or have me ask them, and to give him directives to participate in the session more "appropriately." I encouraged them not to do this; instead, we kept talking and let Matt do what he wanted in the office. As we talked we also observed Matt's actions and reflected on what they might mean.

Resisting the parental reflex to direct, manage, teach, remind, cajole, encourage, reprimand, correct—the list goes on—and focus instead on observing and thinking about our kids is often one of the first things I urge parents to do. The image at the start of this book of the child climbing on the jungle gym while his parent sits at the side ready to witness his efforts and validate his experience illustrates how important this minding function is. But in this high-pressure, obligated-parent climate it's often the first thing to go.

Child development researchers have long stressed the importance of this observational function of parents and linked it to the growth of a robust sense of self in children. At the Hincks-Dellcrest Centre, where I work, clinicians have developed an internationally recognized parent–child therapy called "Watch, Wait and Wonder." We instruct parents to play with their child by following their child's lead, then help them observe and reflect on the meaning of the play. The therapy significantly improves not only the parent–child relationship but emotional and behavioral problems as well.

In an application of this approach, I worked with a wilderness program taking impoverished inner-city families on outdoor excursions where the unique setting provided a perfect opportunity for parents to observe their children and see them in a new light. It was remarkable to watch how quickly these families—many of them experiencing chronic conflict and unhappiness—found their way to a more pleasurable way of being together and how quickly these children, many of them usually quite difficult to manage, settled down into an agreeable and happy mode.

When I encourage parents to step back from micromanaging their kids—something I do on a regular basis these days—I often get the response: "You mean you want me just to do nothing?"

"No," I explain, "I want you to do something, but something that's much harder than the active things—reminding, directing, etc.—that you're used to doing. I want you to pay attention, to observe your child and to try to understand what she is experiencing." For many parents, it takes a while to realize that minding their children really is doing something.

This is what I encouraged Cameron and Beth to do as we sat in my office with Matt. As we continued to talk about the family and some of the unhappy times, Cameron noticed that when Matt did speak, he used a "babyish" tone. Was this Matt's way of coping with the stressful situation he found himself in?

Meanwhile, Beth observed how strongly she felt the need to redirect Matt, despite my instructions. She admitted she was a "micromanager" and that while this had proven effective at her job, perhaps it wasn't so effective at home.

They came on their own the next week. They'd taken to heart my instruction to "watch, wait and wonder" (as opposed to respond, manage and control). Cameron had noticed Matt's voice had become more babyish several times and took this as a possible sign that he was stressed and struggling to cope. Having made an effort to "stop micromanaging," Beth realized just how often she had stepped in to organize and direct.

Today, we don't label kids like Matt "monsters," but we do often label them. Oppositional Defiant Disorder, or ODD, is the label Matt would receive in most diagnostic settings. This may sound less demonizing and more technical than "monster," but it would be just as much a disservice to him. The problem is that it locates the problem in Matt, rather than the context he is acting within. Beth and Cameron agreed to view the problem as systemic, to see Matt's defiance as a logical response to a world that indulged his reluctance to accept things he didn't like.

"He needs a big fat reality check," said Cameron. And he was right.

Too Much of a Good Thing

Today, we know so much about children and childhood development that we can easily forget how novel many of the things are that we "naturally" do with our children. It would be wrong to say that parents didn't love their children in the past—no doubt they did—but the way we think about children today is dramatically different. Actually, that we think about them at all is a change: not only were children left to their own devices much of the time in past societies, but adults didn't spend a lot of time trying to understand them. Certainly, our current knowledge of how deeply early experiences shape an individual would have been unfathomable before the modern age.

Today, the idea that children are entitled to a world that protects and supports their development is one of our society's most cherished values, and our models of child development deeply reflect this. The development of a "secure attachment," for example, in which children develop the confident expectation that a caregiver will be available to meet their needs has been shown to be a central component of healthy emotional growth. Research on "attachment theory" has shown that kids whose parents are reliably available to them are at significantly less risk of developing social and emotional problems, both in childhood and later in life. Children who develop insecure attachments must find other strategies for getting their parents' help and attention. These strategies persist into adulthood, with insecure attachments continuing to cause social and emotional problems.

It's no coincidence that our secular, family-centered and entitled society specializes in parent–child attachment. A sense of entitlement is central to the formation of a secure attachment. A child is securely attached precisely when he no longer has to wonder or worry about a caregiver's availability; when he is able to take his caregiver for granted. In fostering a secure attachment in our children, we are actually creating in our kids a sense of entitlement to our parental resources. We want our children, at least at first, to take us for granted. And insofar as they do, they are able to explore the world and enjoy what it has to offer. A secure attachment is indeed a wonderful thing, and the sense of entitlement is at its heart: "I am special and have a special claim on the universe." When toddlers know they are the center of their parents' universe, they feel emotionally safe. The challenge is to raise securely attached kids, but not allow this attachment to become an entitled, disengaged immaturity.

Clearly, there can be too much of a good thing. As children develop, they need to experience disappointment and privation, little by little, according to their developmental capacity. This, after all, is how a person develops resiliency.

At a certain point in a child's development, say around age 6, a mother who is afraid to leave her son alone with his upset feelings, and either gives in to his tantrums or spends "time-in" with him, is not really helping. Her emotional availability is based on good intentions, but her need for him to be okay—emotionally unscarred—hampers her ability to judge when he really needs her and when she should leave him alone. Explaining decisions and spending time with a misbehaving child fosters a respectful, collaborative relationship and avoids feelings of rejection. But many parents feel so obligated to respond correctly, to use the right strategies at the right time, to not mess up their kid that it becomes difficult for them to maintain a position of authority. Kids can smell their fear, and as soon as they do, the obligated parent will lose the power struggle.

Ironically, the way to regain authority is by letting go. Children actually need parents, so when we stay out of their way but remain attentive and interested, they must deal with the challenges of life and so turn to us. And this, of course, is the position we really want to be in. Because they need us, they listen to us.

Stories of Woe

Cameron and Beth's sense of obligation to attend to their kids and to help at all costs was deep indeed. Part of the problem was that they, like so many contemporary parents, had implicitly adopted the idea that any suffering was bad for a child, and that any hardship that could be avoided, should be avoided. If it wasn't, and they could have prevented it, they would feel directly at fault. The power of this idea and its unhelpful consequences became clear as they began to set firmer limits.

One day, after one of Matt's particularly egregious outbursts, his parents sent him to his room. Though he protested and fought them on this, they used their newfound determination and stuck to their guns, eventually getting him upstairs. Matt of course was upset about this punishment and when, later, Beth went upstairs to check on him, she found yellow sticky notes pasted about the second floor—on his door frame, by the bathroom sink, on his mom's bedside table. "I'm a bad swimmer," said one. "I'm a bad speller," said another. The notes alarmed Beth. She worried about Matt feeling so badly and about his "self-esteem." She worried about depression. She quickly gathered the notes and went to talk to Matt and attempted to "cajole" him out of his low mood.

We examined this together: Beth thought about her need to cajole Matt into a good mood. Where did that come from? She'd seen the notes, and they'd made her worried. Had he left them intentionally? Matt could be manipulative, they agreed, and would often use dramatics to get his way.

"He sucked me in," she concluded, mostly mad at herself.

Well, not totally. Matt was conveying a real hurt—he was sad to be in trouble with his parents, and to the extent that he was hurting it was helpful for Beth to be emotionally available to him. But that's not all that was going on here. With his sticky notes, he was soliciting his mother's caring nature, looking to recruit her, to bring her back to him—an attachment strategy, if you will. And the transparency of his efforts has an immature quality to it. Matt is 8, but in this moment he is regressing to an earlier mode of functioning. He's being a bit babyish.

In succeeding with this strategy, Matt reassured himself of his emotional control over his mother and brought down his anxiety over his behavior. Manipulating would be the dirty word for what he was doing. No matter what word we give such behavior, it wasn't helpful for Beth to respond so gratifyingly.

She didn't have to ignore the notes altogether, though. Once a child has served his punishment, there's nothing to be gained by continuing to be an ogre about it. It's fine to let it go. But in accepting his invitation wholeheartedly, Beth signaled a great deal more.

When our children come to us with a "Story of Woe," there are always two different things going on. The child is conveying a real hurt—and the parent should respond to it. But he's also looking to recruit the parent in some way, to manipulate her—and she should not respond in ways that encourage him. It's always both: sometimes the real hurt is primary, but at other times, as with Matt's sticky notes, it's mostly about the manipulation. Matt really does feel sad—he's been sent away, he's been bad and he knows it and it doesn't feel good. The sadness is real. But so is his attempt to recruit his mother. He wants to reassure himself both of her love for him and his control over her. If he can win her back to his side, regain her compassion and patience, he can reassure himself that all is right with the universe and forget about all the unpleasantness of the previous hour. He can undo it, and pretend it never happened.

Because both things are going on, Beth must tread carefully. She needs to be sympathetic to the hurt and she should tell him that all's forgiven. But she can't be too gratifying. Matt relies on parental control to cope with emotional adversity and this is not healthy. He needs to be "left with his hurt" just enough that he is forced to cope and realize that when you act like a jerk, crappy things happen to you.

Chapter Two

Almost all parents get this right with physical hurts: when her toddler goes *whump* and looks up, ready to scream, Mom is likely to acknowledge the fall but also downplay her concern. She knows that too much concern or too much immediate sympathy will actually elicit more tears and clinging. And Mom wants to discourage this in the interests of the child. If the kid can't handle that little fall, he's going to have trouble dealing with the big, bad world out there. But our generation of parents, anxiously focused on our child's emotional development, sometimes forgets this basic parental wisdom when it comes to the emotional knocks of the world.

In this sense, Beth's attempts to cajole Matt out of his sadness is like the mom who overreacts to the toddler's fall—"Oh, baby!"—and invites the child to erupt into tears. Cameron and Beth's new perspective on their family and Matt's behavior felt liberating: they began to realize just how hard they had been working at things and why. Letting go allowed them to relax and enjoy the family, and each other, more.

The family's daily life improved steadily over the next few weeks. Unless it seemed someone might get seriously hurt, Cameron and Beth ignored the boys' fights. At first, this was "weird for everybody," and Beth struggled with a powerful sense of neglecting her children the first time she stayed in the kitchen as the boys rumbled upstairs. Colin came down in tears looking for her with a deep grievance about Matt's aggression; Matt trailed behind holding out his forearm to show the "red mark." Telling the story, she laughed as the childish absurdity of the situation occurred to her. In the heat of the moment, she'd felt her anxiety rising sharply, but she fought off the powerful impulse to do what she would normally do: question them carefully about the incident and then provide lectures and admonishments.

Instead, she listened to them both, said, "Uh huh" and kept on making dinner.

"Aren't you going to do something?" demanded an incensed Matt. But eventually the two boys wandered off and the fighting diminished in frequency and intensity.

Beth called her new approach "tough love" because that's how it felt to her. "You're responsible for your own lunch bag now," she told her sons, and let them experience the painful failure of not having it at school if they forgot it. It took surprisingly little time for the message to sink in. One day, as they were leaving the house, Matt remembered that he'd borrowed a book from the vice-principal and, as his parents watched in amazement, ran back inside for it. Cameron and Beth also backed off on the nagging about homework and pretty soon, Matt started to ask them for help with his homework. They had passed the worry ball.

DO pay attention

Watching your kids grow up—witnessing their struggles and their failures and successes, seeing them for who they are—is the most important parenting responsibility of them all. Although this sounds simple, it may be the hardest thing a parent has to do these days. With all the social and cultural pressure not to fail our children, the default position for most parents is to be actively involved: guiding, directing, overseeing, reminding, encouraging, cajoling and on and on. As valuable as these instrumental functions are, particularly in the early years, they stand in opposition to the all-important minding role: standing back and letting your child explore, experiment and learn while you pay attention and enjoy the show. By continually intervening, you may bring your own anxiety down by ensuring your child's immediate comfort and success, but you send the implicit message that you don't believe he or she can do it without your help.

Let your child take the lead. In the early years, let him show you how to play and what to play at. Follow where his mind goes, letting him know by your responses that you get him, and like to play along. As he matures, continue to watch and be interested, sending the message that you believe he can do it and that the mistakes he makes along the way are all just part of the process. Continually remind yourself that if you watch carefully enough you will see things in your kids that you haven't seen before, but if you only look for what you expect to see, or fear to see, that is all you will ever see.

DON'T always help

If we stop to watch ourselves, we'll see that we all help our kids do things for all kinds of reasons, especially fears that they won't do it, or won't do it well. So parents get sucked into worrying about getting projects finished or forgetting mittens, even though the natural consequences of avoiding a school project or forgetting your mittens are powerful teachers. There are other reasons for helping, too; for example, I'm often motivated by the simple wish to get it done faster and put it behind me. My young children need a bag of diversions for the endless car ride to Winnipeg? Do I let them figure it out to the extent they can, maybe adding a piece at the end after reviewing their efforts (the right choice)? Or do I do it for them so it's done and they don't forget something critical that might save us an ugly meltdown 500 miles down the road? This was the all-too-common choice for me, and while it ensured that we had the right number of headphones to keep peace between the children, it also kept me in the role of custodian of peace in the car—the obligated parent watching his kids act younger and younger in the back seat. And we're only at Sault Ste. Marie.

DO play with your child

Make sure you find time for play and a chance to have fun together. In the early years, especially, try to let your child lead the play and don't get too hung up on rules. This is play, after all, and 4-year-olds sometimes don't care about rules. It might be more fun for a 4-year-old—certainly better than continuing to lose at a game of checkers—to build a Super King checker with special powers. Okay, the game just changed, but coming up with ways to fend off Super King checkers can be fun, too.

What? And allow him to avoid the painful reality of losing? Yes, because this isn't reality, this is play. If there are other children playing, then following rules is important because then we're dealing with social reality, but when you're playing one-on-one with your young child, you are, in a certain sense, letting him create a world for you to join. Don't worry, if the Super King totally crushes your pathetic attempt to fight back with a Robo Checker and utterly destroys you, he'll bring you right back. It's guaranteed: he'll want to do it again.

This kind of play does no end of good. It strengthens your relationship with your child and helps him organize his own experience by representing his thoughts and feelings in symbolic form. Your playful response sends the message, "Yes, I get it. You want to feel powerful and invincible; you don't like to get pushed around. That's normal." Such experiences actually help children develop better emotional control in the long run.

Three

"I Don't Want to Grow Up"

Judy and David were concerned about the chaos in their home and their sense of powerlessness in the face of their daughter's defiance. Eleven-year-old Tanya was particularly worrisome, though they also struggled with Toby, who was three years younger. The parents described Tanya as a difficult, argumentative child who continually opposed their rules and requests, provoked her brother and created a certain amount of havoc and unhappiness not only at home but also at school and in the community. They were concerned about her moods because she could become frighteningly angry, while at other times she spoke unhappily about things: how mean people were to her, how horrible her life was.

She was a bright and adept child. Attractive, with curly blonde hair and a whole lot of energy, Tanya had been a force to be reckoned with from day one. At first, this had been just fine. In fact, for the first three years of Tanya's life, her bright, eager demeanor brought Judy and David almost nothing but pleasure. During her toddler years she was indeed the center of their universe, and if they were aware that she more or less ran the show at home they implicitly agreed to ignore it for the time being.

It was worth it. For David, who had lost his mother as a child and had an emotionally remote relationship with his father, Judy and the children were all the family he'd ever had. He was a big man with a quiet, gentle manner who did well in his business, which took him out of the house during weekdays. When he wasn't at work, he spent his time with his children, running errands (assigned by Judy), and frequently "snuggling" on the couch with the kids. He had warm, close relationships with them. Indeed, when Tanya was not fighting with her parents, she was often affectionate and even "cuddly." The first years of his daughter's life, when it was just the three of them, were the happiest David had ever known.

When Tanya was 3 and Toby was born, things changed. The introduction of this demanding sibling was a rude interruption to the little girl's world; power struggles began, as did a new level of rage at her parents. And Tanya's sibling rivalry with her brother began as well. By the time the family came to me, she was taking up a great deal of her parents' energy. "We love her to death," Judy told me, "but I think she's going to be the death of us. She soaks up all this love—she can never get enough."

This was a close family. Judy had a strong, forceful personality and she poured herself into parenting with efficient, unceasing care and attention to detail. She described herself as a "micromanager" and though she admitted to being a "screamer and yeller," she was, she told me, "always there for the kids." She and David "put everything we have into the kids and the family," so they rarely socialized or went out. With more than a faint hint of pride, she declared, "I make sure I'm there all the time."

But when life in the family wasn't happy and close, it tended to be very bad. Mornings were entirely dominated by the task of "getting Tanya moving." She required numerous requests to get out of bed, get dressed and get on with the normal morning tasks. Her parents explained that they gave her pancakes every morning because if they didn't, there was no chance of getting her moving at all. Nighttimes were just as bad as they fought over bathing, teeth brushing and bedtimes: "We fight every night with the kids." Getting Tanya to sit and eat dinner was always a challenge and Judy was constantly searching for food that was acceptable to her. Just about everything was a potential struggle or even a fight. And so, just like Matt's parents, Judy and David lived on perpetual eggshells, wondering if Tanya would protest and defy them, while hoping and praying that she would go along with things without incident.

Outside the home she tended to do well when starting out, but she inevitably got into clashes with her peers. School, sports teams, playing in the neighborhood: already Tanya had developed a reputation in all of her worlds—difficult, troubled, a "pain." When it came to actual schoolwork, she did the absolute minimum, but when it came to other aspects of school—a class play, for example—she engaged quite passionately, though often with unfortunate outcomes. Tanya took up a lot of space. Not surprisingly, her friendships tended to be fractious and short-lived.

She often complained about the unfair behavior of others— that she'd been bullied at school and the teacher had not done anything, that her friends weren't nice, that her teacher was mean. "Everyone," she insisted, "is against me."

Judy and David found it hard to evaluate the truthfulness of Tanya's reports about the outside world. They tended to believe her because they wanted to take her seriously and respectfully and to be available and to keep her safe. But they also knew she tended to exaggerate and to distort and, when it came to schoolwork she "lied constantly." Often, they found themselves doubting her unhappy tales of being treated unfairly, or at least doubting their complete truth, but they were afraid to upset her by questioning her too much. She could be volatile, and when she came home with her Stories of Woe, they knew they were on a thin edge, needing to respond with the requisite amount of sympathy because any failure to be perfectly supportive would lead to a quick and angry reaction.

Her teacher's take on Tanya in the classroom was quite different from what the parents expected. She said the girl was "quite buddy-buddy" with Cayley, the child that Judy and David believed was "bullying" her. She described Tanya as "extremely competitive" and something of a "show-off." She agreed that Tanya was bright but noted that the girl put in minimum effort toward her work, just trying to finish the task as quickly as possible, and tended to struggle when required to work independently. Her teacher saw Tanya as a "strong character" who "argued about rules," "looks confident" and acted "like a leader out there." She did not see Tanya as particularly anxious, and certainly not depressed. And when she heard Judy and David's view of their daughter, she said she did not believe Tanya was "under the power of others, a victim or pushed around." Instead, she described her as "sharp and maybe manipulative."

The parents felt helpless. They received no shortage of advice, though. Judy's sister and mother, especially, never hesitated to offer input and observations: take her to a tutor, get her assessed for ADHD, spend more time with her doing her homework. All the advice was at least implicitly, and often explicitly, judgmental and anxiety-inducing.

At home, as their stress over Tanya increased, they felt their leverage—their capacity to get her to focus on the things she should—slipping. They bargained with her and in their desperation they gave in to demands such as, "I'll do my stupid assignment if you let me have Facebook."

When Tanya's behavior was truly egregious, the parents provided a reasonably balanced "consequence." Once, when the car was packed and running in the driveway, ready to leave on the family holiday, Tanya refused to leave her room because she hadn't been guaranteed the front seat. Judy and David dealt with it finally by allowing her to sit in the front seat as they left the house on the first leg of the trip, on the understanding that they were "grounding" her at a later date. But these consequences and, more often, the threats of consequences, were increasingly ineffective. In fact, this approach was actually feeding their sense of powerlessness.

An 11-year-old girl shouldn't have to be grounded on a holiday for refusing to get in the car, but the more they relied on the consequence system the more they faced the absurd behavior. Now it seemed the only way Tanya would ever cooperate was if they had sufficient leverage (a big enough threat or a big enough bribe); it seemed entirely out of the question that she would ever obey just because they said so. The more they used consequences, the more they became dependent on them. And Tanya sensed that her parents' tactics smacked of desperation: she smelled their fear.

The Problem of Reality

Tanya was not dealing with important parts of reality. She didn't really give schoolwork a second thought, except when a good result might gain her status in her peer group; instead, she did the minimum and her main concern was getting her parents and teacher off her back. But, of course, the reality is: school is important and our kids need to make an effort if they want to succeed in life. Her parents were forever broadcasting that message in one way or another, but it was all just white noise to Tanya. The nagging was an irritant that she ignored much of the time, but occasionally, when it grew loud enough, she had to deal with it directly. She did just enough work to get everyone to shut up.

She also hated to lose and often left games and social interactions if she didn't succeed quickly. But the reality is: sometimes we don't get things our way and we have to deal with our own limitations. To a worrying degree, Tanya lived in denial of this. She lacked the capacity to tolerate disappointment and the shock of her own limitations. Hers was a black-and-white world where she was either popular and "the best" (she always hung with the coolest kids or she didn't hang at all), or she left, retreating to her home life and complaining about the world out there where people are "unfair," "mean" and "don't like her."

As a result, her perspective on events was often different from that of others. Once, when not getting her way with classmates working on a project, she sabotaged the group's work when the teacher was out of the room. Tanya's version was that the kids "ganged up on her." When her parents pushed her a little bit, pointing out that she had also misbehaved, she shamelessly added, "Well, Cayley smashed the model." She delivered the lie with apparently complete conviction that it was the truth.

As a hyper competitive show off, her behavior had a tendency to, in her teacher's words, "set the other kids off." She lacked the awareness of her more mature peers that allowed them to come off well and appear likeable to each other. She was boastful, given to fabrications and exaggerations, and reluctant, perhaps even unable, to feel happy for others' successes. She felt envy as opposed to appreciation. But the reality is: we all must leave space for our peers, give them a chance to be in the limelight, share things and tolerate not being the best or the center of attention at all times. Tanya was struggling with this important step.

Because Judy and David were the voice of reality in the family, they had to remind Tanya about her studies, structure her homework time (or at least try to) and give her pep talks and carefully worded lectures on the importance of a variety of subjects: "putting in a good effort," "trying," not being rude, sharing—the list went on. Her parents were certainly oriented toward reality. They thought about it, worried about it and planned by looking ahead; they just needed to get Tanya with the program. But the girl didn't need to focus on reality because her parents were so clearly and busily doing it for her. And who'd really want to? So she devoted her not inconsiderable abilities to working her parents: appeasing them, getting them off her back, but also getting them to give her what she wanted. Basically, bending them to her will. She was focused on her immediate desires— this gadget, that piece of clothing, the TV show that didn't end until 11 p.m., a weeknight sleepover.

Tanya employed various strategies to keep her parents under her control. She made threats—"I'm not leaving unless you say I can sleep at Bridgit's tonight"—and she followed through on these often enough to cow her parents. She was adept at scaring them because she'd figured out what they feared and threatened them with it. "Fine, then, I'm not doing my spelling!" she'd say, relying on their fears about school to light a fire under them. This cut-off-your-nose-to-spite-your-face strategy is a common one, but it made Judy and David so anxious that they inevitably backed down.

Tanya had ensured her parents carried the worry ball. They fretted about spelling and math, about proper diet and enough sleep, about brushing teeth and avoiding cavities. They stressed about her mood, her friendships and getting her into a good private school in a few years. Their worry kept them instrumentally involved in Tanya's life: organizing, managing, reminding, encouraging, teaching, guiding, directing, overseeing—a long inventory of active parenting functions they were afraid to drop. But these actions were so different from the minding function: sitting on the park bench, separate but interested, not overly involved but available for accidents and the recognition of achievements.

This seemed their only choice. If they stopped, it seemed clear, Tanya would slip and fall. Bad things would happen: if they didn't remind her what to take with her, she'd forget it; if they didn't tell her to do it, she wouldn't do it. And she would suffer the unfortunate results, they feared, such as missing the field trip, being unable to go to gym class without her shoes, going hungry. And if they weren't perfectly sympathetic when she was clearly distressed, who knows what could happen? Maybe it would just be too much for her. Judy and David were so anxiously focused on Tanya that they couldn't bear to let her suffer these painful, yet non-catastrophic, consequences.

The Terrible Twos

Peter Pan was onto something we all feel at times: growing up means taking on the world, shouldering responsibility and accepting harsh realities. When you're just starting out, you have yet to encounter reality, let alone accept it. Imagine Tanya over her first year, gradually making sense of the world around her, taking in its sights and sounds, registering the faces of the important people around her (information of special importance to the infant brain), and exploring her own body and its capacities. Over that year, she learned much: to communicate, to sit up, to crawl, to lie down, to laugh, to cry. And when, likely toward the end of her first year, she developed the capacity to walk and move herself independently around the world, she entered a new age of exploration. By the time she was 18 months or so, Tanya would have been able to move herself around pretty well, discovering the many wonders and delights the world has to offer. We can imagine her days, filled with excitement, joy and pleasure.

This time in a child's development has been called a "love affair with the world." It's an idyllic time when each new moment holds potential delights. Life is great because someone feeds you and takes you to the park and lets you play with toys and see new sights: "A doggie! Look at the doggie!" You're cute, so everyone loves you, and other people take care of all your needs, so you don't need to worry about a thing. Truly, the world is your oyster.

Until it isn't. Because, inevitably, reality eventually roars in and you realize your idyllic world has limits. Suddenly, it's time to go home for dinner and you were just starting to play in the sandbox and you don't want to go home. You can't have that chocolate bar. Someone loud barks at you: "Don't do that!" "Don't go there!" "Don't touch that!" And sometimes—this is worst of all—you're left alone: in your crib at night or just left (at the daycare or with a sitter). This can be the harshest reality check of all: you are separate from Mom and Dad, you are an individual and sometimes you must be alone.

The first response to this gross affront to freedom and desire—the absolute heart of all the "terribleness" of many 2-year-olds—is to oppose it and deny it and go for control. The toddler in the shopping cart who wants a sweet and reaches out for it, only to be told she can't have it, throws a tantrum. If her parents stay firm, as they know they should, they may well enjoy an escalation, often an embarrassing escalation, as she has a "complete meltdown." The kid is down on the floor, shrieking, kicking her heels and going red in the face. The grief and rage, the apparent out-of-control-ness of some of these displays, seem way out of proportion to parents. "Geez, it was just that shiny thing in the cooking section. I can't see why it's such a big deal." But it's no longer about the chocolate bar or the shiny thing in the cooking section. It's about, "I can't have my way."

This aspect of the 2-year-old's tantrum is important to understand. These outbursts can seem so much greater than the situation warrants because they quickly become about something much more than chocolate bars. They are about having to face the reality that she can't order the world the way she wants, and that she can't solve the problem of reality by controlling Mom.

A natural battle of wills breaks out between the toddler and her parents, who must set limits, anticipate danger and stick to daily routines. Reality, it turns out, sucks. And parents are the first people to deliver that news to their children: "No, it's time to go," "No, you can't play with that" and "No, you can't have another cookie." So children, who have an understandable wish to go for control over their parents, direct their first rage at them.

But here's the problem: if the temper tantrums prove successful, the child will no doubt do it again, and if successful, will no doubt continue to throw them in the future—and move on to other forms of defiance and naughtiness.

Tanya had long been a challenge for her parents. It was as if she'd hit the terrible twos and never came out of it. I could just imagine her at 2: radiant, adorable, insatiable. To Judy and David her pleasure in the world and the glowing response she must have got back from it would have been a constant delight. They likely seldom felt inclined to limit her, being happy to follow along and enjoy the show. This came to a crashing halt with the arrival of Toby and suddenly she no longer occupied the central place she previously had in the family, and which she'd taken for granted. That's when the battles really began. Since then, they'd had to work extra hard to get her to leave the playground, eat her dinner and go to bed. And so, from early on, they'd found themselves resorting to consequences such as taking away her toys and threatening to cancel upcoming events. As she got older, the battles changed: getting up in time to go to school, turning off the computer, not tormenting her brother. So did the consequences: unplugging computers, threatening to take away the TV time, restricting access to play dates if homework wasn't done.

These battles had taken on an increasingly desperate tone. It wasn't that Judy and David were particularly bad at following through on their threats—they often did—it just seemed as though they'd become locked in a never-ending battle of wills with their daughter. And it was always an open question how Tanya would behave on any given occasion.

Power Struggles

In this age of obligated parents and entitled children, power struggles like the one Judy and David found themselves in with Tanya are increasingly common. Often, by the time these families come to me the struggle has taken on a darker edge, with children being rude and hurtful, sometimes doing or saying the most upsetting things—being beyond disrespectful. Tanya's parents worried about this in her: was this some malignant part of her personality? They didn't use the term, but given that her actions often seemed to lack concern for others and at times just seemed downright mean, they feared she had antisocial tendencies.

But as we looked at Tanya's behavior in light of this parent–child tangle, driven by their powerful sense of parental obligation, we began to see how these antisocial tendencies didn't so much reside in Tanya as in the family system she lived and operated within, a system in which control had taken on a prime significance. In this family, each side tried to find leverage to assert control. Tanya used scare tactics: "Fine, I'm not going to study for my test then," while Judy and David used the threat of consequences: "If you don't study for the test, you're not going to dance class tomorrow." And as this struggle continued, both sides felt increasingly uneasy about the idea of relinquishing control, so the struggle became more desperate, the threat of "losing" became more real and their efforts to win (gain control) became greater.

Young children approach this power struggle much differently than mentally healthy adults do. One of the main differences, from an emotional point of view, is the child's dependency on the parent, and the problems this creates, beginning with the terrible twos. At that age, as the mother begins to disappoint and frustrate her child, as inevitably she must, he is painfully reminded of his vulnerability, his separateness from her and his potential emotional dependence on her.

Why is this dependency on the parent such a problem for the toddler? Well, for one thing it's highly inconvenient and frustrating, especially when the parent disappoints. But beyond this—deeper than this, you might say—the child is dependent on the parent for his psychological survival. Recall our jungle gym example, where the child turns to Mom for recognition ("Look at me!"). This moment isn't just good for kids, it's absolutely essential. Children who grow up without such parental attention—children who grow up in certain orphanages, for example—are destined for lives with severe emotional, relational and behavioral problems. For children to develop a clear and solid sense of who they are, and a confident sense that they have a place in the world, they require consistent parental attention and emotional attunement. That's why being on the park bench, watching the child on the play structure, is so crucial.

But it also adds a whole other level to the child's dependency. The toddler isn't just dependent on Mom for the chocolate bar and longer stays in the park, he is dependant on her for his very existence, including his sense of self-worth and security in the world. He needs her desperately, but his desperate need is terrifying, so he denies it. And this is precisely why the "twos" can be so "terrible" sometimes. As he slowly moves into toddlerhood, exploring unfolding possibilities and personal capacities, the child's dawning awareness of his need for his mother deeply threatens his fragile sense of autonomy, because if he needs her, then he is not actually free. If he needs her, then he is vulnerable. The problem for the toddler is that he needs his mother to validate his strivings and to recognize him, he needs his mother to help him meet his needs. Yet, he must deny this dependency and the vulnerability it entails.

This ushers in an ambivalent stage of early childhood development—dubbed the "rapprochement crisis"—during which he wishes to both cling to a parent and to push her away. In a now-famous 1965 study using an observational nursery, researchers led by Margaret Mahler watched groups of mothers and their toddlers spend the day together. Their summary of the behavior of the 18- to 24-month-olds describes the children's ambivalence nicely, their simultaneous wish to have Mom all the time and in every way, and to deny her importance: "[The toddlers were] quite eager to exercise their rapidly growing autonomy to the hilt. Increasingly, they chose not to be reminded that at times they could not manage on their own. Conflicts ensued that seemed to hinge upon the desire to be separate, grand, and omnipotent, on the one hand, and to have mother magically fulfill their wishes, without their having to recognize that help was actually coming from the outside, on the other. In more cases than not, the prevalent mood changed to that of general dissatisfaction, insatiability, a proneness to rapid swings of mood and to temper tantrums."

What is so striking about this description is how character-istic it could be of current parent–child relationships at almost any age, including teenagers and even "adult children." We could easily insert the words "The teenagers were . . ." at the beginning of the quotation and we would be describing some-thing familiar to a lot of parents: teens insistent on their own autonomy, oblivious to the costs and inconveniences to others, entitled to having their wishes fulfilled.

When I see power struggles between teenagers and their parents, many of the terms have changed but the basic dynamics remain the same. Like Tanya, they will angrily defy and disre-spect their parents in one moment, and then turn to them, fully expecting them to deliver the goods, the next moment. This is the brazen sense of personal entitlement that Anthony Wolf captures in the title of his excellent book on the subject, *Get Out of My Life, but First Could You Drive Me and Cheryl to the Mall?*

One of the reasons it's so important to get it right during the terrible twos is what you get wrong then will haunt you later. By the time I met Judy and David, this power struggle seemed to have developed a life of its own. Tanya, a teen in the mak-ing, couldn't stop herself from challenging them, defying them and, at times, being ugly and rude to them. They loved the time when things were close and warm—Tanya always found ways to initiate snuggles, especially if her parents were upset with her—and she could disarm them with a snuggle attack, undo their dissatisfaction and restore the family status quo. With her in control. At other times, she defied them and caused the family all kinds of inconvenience. It really felt like Tanya was in control most of the time. The sense of being a slave to Tanya's master was powerful for both Judy and David, as it is for many of the parents I meet in this predicament, with kids of almost any age.

Master and Slave

Like Tanya, 6-year-old Trevor was a child who was set on controlling his parents, particularly his mother. And like Tanya, he frequently opposed the rules, provoked conflict and demanded that he get what he wanted, refusing to cooperate if he didn't. In Trevor's case, however, his parents, Sarah and Kyle, were separated and his relationship with his mother provides a powerful illustration of how a power struggle can trap both parent and child in a cycle that neither can "win." If there was ever a child who seemed like an imperious tyrant to his parents, it was Trevor.

By their own admission, his parents were "wusses" with their kids; they had had a hard time setting limits and sticking with them. After their separation and divorce, when Trevor was 4 and his younger brother Dylan was 2, Sarah had even more difficulty establishing order in her own home. Because she had a reflexive need not to be "mean," she acknowledged that she often didn't know when to "cut it off" or be "strict." Trevor rejected a meal she'd prepared, so she found herself producing several alternatives—and when none of those were successful, she made him oatmeal. "I forgot what I was doing," she said, referring to her loss of perspective—and therefore control over her actions—as she was swept up in the powerful interplay between child and parent. "I'm a jellyfish parent, and they're knocking the crap out of me," Sarah admitted. "I give them everything and they're rude and disrespectful."

Still, she worried about hurting or traumatizing her kids and felt a need to "make up for the split." She had a deep sense of guilt that the divorce had damaged them and she needed to redress the damage. Her greatest fear was that "they won't love me." This led Sarah to be overly permissive and the result was that Trevor ran the show at his mother's house.

He tended to be quite possessive of his mother, begrudging the time she spent with little Dylan. Sarah had become adept at finding ways to nurture Dylan, on the fly as it were, while managing Trevor. The older boy particularly loved his collection of small plush toys, to which he was constantly adding or demanding new acquisitions (at just six-and-a-half years old, he could find them on the Internet). He had one particular favorite, a green frog named Ribbit, with whom he would sometimes plague the family. The name came from the fact that the frog said "ribbit," and sometimes said it a lot. Ribbit would often end up in Mom's or Dylan's face "ribbiting," much to their irritation. When Ribbit appeared, Trevor would become more babyish, and Ribbit often talked in a baby voice.

Sarah could usually find a way to redirect Trevor at these times. Trevor would turn Ribbit into a storyteller, and regale his mother and little brother with crazy stories—sometimes funny, sometimes disturbing—about Ribbit's life: How he married Mommy and then divorced Mommy; how he married Dylan. His stories often seemed deliberately provocative and his audience felt more trapped than anything, knowing that if they didn't pay attention they might get more ribbiting, or worse.

When he was unhappy with how things went at school or out in the community, Trevor would dramatize his hurt in various ways, making statements about his unhappiness and suffering, and over-the-top exhibitions of how upset he was. To the outside observer, these efforts were transparent, but they were often effective—Sarah couldn't see through them. But Kyle, Trevor's father, usually could. His impatience with his ex would often emerge in our sessions together. He saw how easily she could be played, and was aware of how this encouraged regressive, controlling behavior in the kids.

All this power seemed to make Trevor contemptuous of his mother. He often treated her horribly, as if she had somehow devalued herself in his eyes. Trevor often turned angrily on Sarah, blaming her for things he didn't like, or saying accusingly, "You ruined my life!" She knew she should be stricter, but when she was, Trevor would tell her, "I hate you." And then she would back down. Or, if she tried to stay firm, he'd threaten to go to his dad's house. And she would back down.

He bossed her around shamelessly, routinely called her terrible names and, knowing her weak spots, went after them mercilessly. If ever a parent felt slave-like it was Sarah, and as bad as this was for her, it made her even more worried about her son. What would he be like as an adult, she worried? Would he treat his wife like this?

Once again, it was helpful for Kyle and Sarah to understand that this ugly streak did not reside in Trevor, but was an expression of the system—let's call it the master-slave system—in which he operated. Ideally, a child solves his dependency dilemma by discovering, slowly, that he can tolerate some disappointment, as long as it is within manageable limits. When a mother remains outside of her child's omnipotent control, she maintains her value to him as a separate other, capable of recognizing and validating him. American psychoanalyst Jessica Benjamin, in *The Bonds of Love: Psychoanalysis, Feminism, and the Problem of Domination,* her classic study of this dynamic, calls the ideal solution "mutual recognition." The parent (mother) who resists the child's attempts to bend her to his will maintains a kind of personal legitimacy in his world as an independent but caring other. When this happens, the mother is able to continue to give legitimacy to him—she recognizes him and validates his independence; and the child legitimizes his mother as an other—someone who is separate from him, and therefore capable of being loved, valued and (at least at times) listened to.

But, to do this, she must resist the infant's demand to meet his every need and never fail him. She must resist his bid for omnipotence. This is what Sarah struggled to do with Trevor. In regularly acquiescing to his demands, and with her evident need for him to be happy with her, to approve of her with his love and satisfaction, she had devalued herself as an authoritative and emotionally separate other. And now, just like Judy and David with Tanya, she could never seem to give him enough.

"Winning" this battle for control was an empty victory for Trevor. Once he turned to this solution—taking magical control of his mother instead of accepting and dealing with the real world—he had to maintain control over her. He clung to his control of her and was sensitive to any chance that it might be jeopardized, and he angrily resisted anything that reminded him of his lack of autonomy.

Ironically, Trevor's constant focus on getting his way interfered with his actual autonomy and effectively narrowed his world. When I met with him he'd first hide in the waiting room, choosing his own time to enter my office; when sessions were over, he refused to leave, choosing his own time to depart. For a child so set on autonomy, he seemed to have little choice about doing this, as if he were driven to prove himself in control. In our first sessions, Trevor constantly tested the limits of my office (and my patience). Once I'd survived his anxious testing and we settled into playing together, his play revealed an overriding concern with power and control. His team or player was all-powerful, while mine was tiny and pushed around. The rules were clear: you were either strong and on top (Trevor), or weak and on the bottom (me). Either master or slave, there was no in-between.

This is familiar to any play therapist who deals with young children. Boys, especially, work through these early attempts at figuring out who they are and where they stand in the big world. In our games, Trevor would set up his "army" (a collection of play figures, including dinosaurs, action figures and a small Pikachu figure from Pokémon), while I set up mine (less powerful-looking figures: a dolphin, a small female Playmobil figure, a broken, one-legged cowboy action figure—who actually is kind of cool-looking but, let's face it, has only one leg). Then the "war" started. At first, this part of the play was relatively short as Trevor's side quickly pulverized mine, reducing my "base" to a pile of rubble and killing all my guys. Of course, this meant regrouping by rebuilding our bases and starting again—so he could destroy me again. In our first clashes, if I animated any of my figures with even the least bit of aggression or resistance (say, the one-legged cowboy suddenly spun out of the way and attempted a small flying dropkick), I was instantly and furiously crushed.

This repetitive playing out of the scene, so characteristic of play therapy, demonstrated a rather classic dilemma for Trevor: the problem of the obliterated other. Needing to demonstrate his complete superiority over me, the boy was driven not just to beat me, but to utterly destroy me—to reveal my weak puniness while demonstrating his powerful hugeness. But once he'd destroyed me, I was no good to him anymore. So he needed to bring me back, to start again. His problem was he needed me at the same time that he wanted to assert his complete mastery of me—the same dilemma he faced with his mother. And the play, which was fun, was forcing him to recognize this reality, because it was (a little bit) disappointing each time I "died" to discover that it was over; I was no good to him anymore.

Trevor naturally learned to extend the wars to preserve the fun. To do so, he attacked slightly less ferociously, and destroyed me in a more piece-by-piece fashion. He also started to give me better stuff: I was allowed to have two or three "bombs" (marbles) and, surprisingly, at one point, even the tank: it was more fun when I put up a bit more of a fight. (I had more fun too.) And when Trevor found himself enjoying interacting with another who could stand up to him a bit, he actually had more fun. My guys slowly started to be allowed to fight back. We had extended kung fu battles, my one-legged cowboy doing mid-air spin-kicks versus Pikachu riding on a "flying saucer" shooting electric bolts.

Turns out, Trevor wanted out of the master–slave trap just as badly as Sarah.

Gaining Respect

As Rousseau observed 250 years ago about the child whose caregiver will do anything not to fail him: "if he once learns that he can interest you in his case at his own pleasure, he has become your master, and all is lost." When the parent's need to please the child makes her overly vulnerable to his demands, the door is open for him to obtain a level of control that is harmful to his own emotional development. Able to bend his mother to his will, Trevor didn't need to accept the limits of his powers and the limitations inherent in life. This is why children who "win" the battle for omnipotence are not just controlling, they are anxiously controlling. Having avoided the painful awareness of their separateness and vulnerability, these children must continue to assert control.

Knowing she had to be tougher with Trevor, Sarah worked on saying "no" and sticking with it. When he and his brother began to resist and appeal her verdict as usual, she told them, "I'm getting mad." That was something she'd never done before. "They need to respect the rules," she declared.

Sarah initiated a "Loonie morning program": if the kids met their responsibilities—get up, eat breakfast, do things on their own (get dressed, for example), with no complaining—she gave them a loonie. She'd started to insist that the kids carry a bag from the grocery store. The kids continued to battle her. They didn't take to these new rules easily, though they certainly noticed them. They accused her of "changing," of becoming a "witch" and told her, "You used to be so nice."

These words upset Sarah because they went right to the heart of her fears. Still, she was feeling better about the changes she'd made, and better about herself. She resolved to continue to stand firm with the boys. The next time she came in, I joked, "There's a new sheriff in town."

Inevitably, though, a new sheriff will be tested with a shoot-out. One day, Trevor was intentionally provocative and rude after Sarah refused to buy him a new plush toy. Following her new approach, she stayed firm and refused to buy it the next day either, even though Trevor's requests had escalated to demands. After he rebelled, Sarah took away his Nintendo DS and banished him from her presence. Trevor pushed himself at her, in an attempt to get "in her face." He refused to go to his room so, finally, in frustration, Sarah went to her own room and latched the door. Trevor hurled abuse at her and tried to break down the door and eventually caused some minor damage to the door frame.

Basically, he threw a temper tantrum worthy of an 18-month-old. And just as with a boy in the terrible twos, the extraordinary vehemence of this performance was explained by the terrifying reality it presented to Trevor: he wasn't going to be able to rely on the childish strategy of owning Mommy. Sarah had to summon great resolve, but once Trevor had to respect the fact that he couldn't get away with this behavior, he started to lay off the full-frontal attacks.

That's why surrendering to tantrums in the terrible twos is a mistake many parents deeply regret for years after. What is at stake is the child's relationship with reality, including the level of responsibility he is going to take for himself in the world, how much frustration he will be willing to tolerate, how much gratification he will be able to delay and many other vitally important components of resiliency. Because a child first negotiates reality with his parents, the way he works it out with them sets a pattern.

Worse than just getting more cavities from eating too much chocolate, once children win the battle for more chocolate, they set a pattern of avoiding the limitations inherent in life. The child who wins control learns that if she protests, life can be more to her liking. But it also means she increasingly focuses her energy on manipulating her parents, and less on what's really happening in the world around her, about which she cares less and less. And so she gradually falls behind in areas where she must compete and contend with adversity, instead retreating from these experiences back to her original world (her family) where she has a sense of security and can control her parents.

In Judy and David's family, respect was something the parents were looking for as well. Realizing that Tanya's 24-hour-a-day access to them—she would throw herself on Dad whenever her father was on the couch, whether he was ready or not—was not in anyone's interests, Judy and David insisted that Tanya respect their personal space and limits, to ask before just jumping on somebody. She needed to respect them as separate people with their own needs and feelings.

When Tanya tried to sabotage an extended family gathering at their home, the parents deftly shifted the event to a nearby restaurant and Tanya, left at home with a babysitter, sabotaged her room, cutting up a picture of herself with her mom into little pieces and leaving it on her mother's pillow.

Judy realized that the need for respect cut both ways. She was deeply identified with her role as parent and loved not only her kids, but also being a parent. Her habit, accordingly, was to refer to herself in the third person when interacting with her kids: "Mommy needs you to get in the car now." Reflecting on this, she saw that this might be patronizing. "If I want her to grow up, I guess I'd better treat her like she's more grown up."

The issue was larger than Judy's language choices, though. The deep level of control she exercised over the kids—the whole family, in fact—meant that Tanya and her brother had little opportunity to take the initiative on anything. The family's life was scheduled and scripted with Judy playing chief camp counselor every step of the way, whistle around her neck, clipboard in hand, yelling at everyone to get on the bus: wake up, brush teeth, get to school, go to after-school program, do homework, enjoy some supervised screen time, brush teeth, go to sleep. The kids' options were to obey or to resist, neither of which, when the parents thought about it, they wanted. In fact, exercising this level of control confirmed Tanya's sense that she lived in a control-or-be-controlled world. By respectfully letting go of some control, Judy could signal a different worldview, one in which everyone had some autonomy.

Chapter Three

Both Tanya and Trevor had to endure some painful reality checks. When Trevor smashed his mother's door-frame, he was a frantic and unhappy child, as was Tanya when she was left at home because she couldn't behave herself. To paraphrase singer-songwriter Paul Simon, believing they had supernatural powers, they slammed into a brick wall.

The problems may have been similar, but I saw completely different outcomes with these two families. I struggled to help Judy and David, who actually consulted me twice, once when Tanya was 7 and then again when she was 11. The problems were the same both times, and as far as I could see, pretty much unchanged when we last spoke, a bit before Tanya's 12th birthday. One of the things these parents were never able to do, or didn't want to do, was to create a kind of emotional separateness between themselves and their kids. For both of them, their lives were their family, in every way. They didn't want to stop being involved in them. And the frenetic, dramatic, often unhappy but occasionally riotously fun family home was the result.

Sarah, though, recognized the need for this separateness from Trevor, for his sake, his brother's sake and for her sake. She saw this as a fight for respect and she was committed to it. She succeeded in part because the development of respect is, in the end, pleasurable for all.

As Trevor and I got along better and better in our play therapy sessions, I achieved the status of virtual equal. Our wars no longer even ended; the drama extended over the entire session and then we left it in suspended animation for the next time. This play was deeply engaging and rewarding for Trevor, as it was for me, because it included a gratifying interpersonal exchange with someone who, laughingly, gave it right back.

At home, Sarah was more determined than ever, and things improved slowly. She became firmer, but there was still considerable conflict, particularly between the two boys. One common catalyst was Ribbit, who still frequently pestered everyone. In a session with Sarah and both boys in my office, the subject of the toy came up. As we spoke, Trevor took on the voice of Ribbit and Sarah reflected on the similarities between the toy's life (based on all the stories) and Trevor's life: both had experienced marriage and divorce and both loved but sometimes got really mad at Sarah. Trevor settled visibly as Sarah talked, agreeing with her observations. At the end of the session, I asked the boys, "If an angel came to your house tonight and you woke up in the morning and everything in your family was better, what would be different?" Trevor suddenly reverted to his baby voice. "Ribbit gone," he said. "Trevor forget Ribbit."

When I last spoke to Sarah, four months later, she was feeling considerably more in control at home. She understood how her anxiety distorted her "picture" of Trevor and that holding on to this perspective enabled her to "get distance" and "be stronger, be a mother, not a scared girl." Meanwhile, Trevor had matured, leading to a much more enjoyable relationship with his brother. And he hadn't pulled out Ribbit in months. Ribbit gone.

DON'T finger-wag

Finger-wagging is so easy to do. Or perhaps I should put it the other way around: not finger-wagging is hard to do. When your kid has just bombed a French test because he stayed up all night watching vampire movies instead of studying, it's pretty difficult to resist the temptation to step in with a comment—some version of "See what happens . . . ?"—and the more costly the mistake, the greater the urge. But finger-wagging takes his attention off the real world, where he is doing some hard learning, and puts it back onto you.

Sometimes parents will say, "Come on, he's done [name the sin]. I think I have a right to say something." I suggest that whether or not his misconduct deserves your condemnation is irrelevant. Instead, ask yourself how helpful it will be. Pay attention to outcomes. Sometimes your finger-wagging may actually lead to an expression of remorse and acknowledgment from your child, and this is a good thing to the extent that it leads her to do things differently in the future. But the finger-wagging itself—or perhaps more accurately the nature of the parent–child relationship implied by the finger-wagging—often makes this next step slower to happen. This form of the parent–child relationship leads to please-appease mode, at best. At worst, and perhaps most frequently, it triggers a negative, defensive reaction in children who are now more likely to be focused on the inaccuracy or injustice of your finger-wagging position than on really getting down to fixing whatever is going wrong in their lives.

Emotionally, of course, kids are all too ready to hear their parents' finger-wagging anyway: it may be unpleasant, but it's also familiar and preferable to real world stress. So remember, when she screws up, and something painful is happening, she's about to learn. To the extent that you draw her attention to yourself and your displeasure or negative opinion, you're interfering with whatever learning she could be doing at that moment. Instead, be sympathetic and supportive, and don't solve her problem for her.

DO get angry (when appropriate)

Our greater understanding of children's emotional needs and the devastating effects of parental abuse—physical or verbal—has led to a greater sensitivity to parental anger. Many modern, obligated parents will go to great lengths to maintain patience and refrain from losing it with their kids. This is a good thing: after all, you're modeling tolerant, patient behavior. But it can be too much of a good thing. When a 5-year-old has a "terrible two" moment, tyrannizing, provoking, taking it way too far, you're doing the kid a disservice by bending down patiently to his level to say in soft measured tones, "Now, Johnny, when you called Mommy an idiot it hurt my feelings." You're depriving the child of an opportunity to learn some essential information—namely, that when you act like a jerk, people don't like it and they get mad. You can't just say mad at this moment, you have to do mad, genuinely (and within reasonable limits). Without such feedback, your child will definitely continue to be disrespectful until eventually he's a teenager, when he can be genuinely ugly. That's when you'll no longer be able to stay patient and you will yell at him—just when it isn't helpful. Yelling at teenagers never works: it just alienates them. Yelling at younger kids does work: it freaks them out and they don't like it.

Yelling all the time is bad, and losing your temper and yelling hurtful things is always bad. But getting appropriately angry when your child is being too unreasonable, hurtful or uncooperative is actually essential. If you don't, they won't have to respect you as a person, and will continue to treat you as a parenting machine, something they can treat any way they wish because it never really complains.

DON'T sign up to be the referee

Siblings quarrel and fight. Some more than others, but just about all do. Refereeing invites children to squabble more in the future. By consistently accepting the role of limit-setter, you send the implicit message that the kids don't have to learn to set limits for themselves. There's actually a really good reason people don't generally fight and squabble and come to blows with each other on a daily basis—it's highly unpleasant. So this isn't something they should need you to do. If they're fighting, squabbling or arguing, you'll have to just let them go sometimes.

Of course you don't want anyone to get hurt for real, and you need to keep an eye out for power imbalances and ongoing "bullying." For example, when children are very young, they will need you to keep a closer eye on things. A 2- or 3-year-old toddler with a baby sibling who's just a year old are not evenly matched, and 3-year-olds, particularly angry or frustrated ones, cannot yet be expected to always be in control of themselves. So, like everything else, it is a matter of slowly stepping out of the referee and house-supervisor role. Successfully not intervening, as your children grow and their disputes shift and change, will help them to learn how to work things out for themselves.

It's important to create a safe home, where people treat each other respectfully, and there are ways to do that, but no matter how well you do, your children may still bicker. Keeping your own behavior under control is the best way to create a safe home. If you want your children to treat each other respectfully, even when they're upset with each other, you have to make sure you behave that way yourself.

Four

School and the "Looming Conveyor Belt of Life"

Morgan screwed up university. He had no choice but to drop out in the middle of his second year after he came home for Christmas and his parents discovered he hadn't attended any classes since he'd bombed in his midterm exams. So when fellow students returned to classes in January, he stayed behind. He lived in his old room at home and saw friends occasionally, but wasn't really doing much.

By May, his parents were so distressed that they set up an appointment for him to see me. By the time we met, Morgan was feeling ready to talk. The pleasant and attractive 20-year-old had had a rough year and was having to face that fact. He still often felt "fine," he said, but occasionally, and now more frequently, he didn't. "Shitty. Empty. Hollow. Alone." were some of the words he used to describe his mood on those days. Then, after a pause, he added, "Not caring."

He was rather ashamed of what had happened—or not happened—at school and was quick to shake his head at himself and call himself a fool: beating me to the punch, perhaps. He struggled to understand what had gone wrong. "Halfway through, I stopped being able to work, sleeping most of the day. I stopped going to school . . . my friends knew . . . I wasn't eating well, but otherwise I seemed fine."

During the days, he went through the motions of being a university student, partying at night, hanging out with friends. But he lived in a state of denial and found ways to not think about (or feel) what he was—and wasn't—doing. This emotional solution became increasingly precarious. "A couple of times I woke up in a panic sweat, worrying, 'How am I going to tell my parents?'" Finally, it all came out and there was no hiding. Morgan described the day that his parents "found out" as a living hell. He was at home with them, and their astonishment and distress were painful for him to witness.

Despite this pain, the whole situation raised a powerful wave of "not caring" in him. That was Morgan's tried-and-true way of coping. He reported an odd absence of affection toward his parents that had developed since he'd been home. As he talked, he had the unsettling realization that he lacked a sense of attachment to them. "My parents, why don't I feel connected to them? I feel bad about this. No, I don't feel bad about it and I know I should and I think maybe I feel bad about that. That's pathetic. My parents are obviously good people, and here I am not doing anything with my life—and then I end up being bugged by them. I don't show it, but there's no closeness. I know this hurts them. I went to university just to get away. I had to pass for them. I promised them I'd try."

A "failure to launch" if ever there was one, Morgan was struggling to move from childhood to adulthood. He had an idea of what an adult was, he could imagine it, but he didn't feel it. He didn't know how to go from here to there. "I never held down a job of my own. It makes me nervous. How do I get one? I'm in a situation I've never encountered before. I don't know how to act." So, much like the little boy who fantasizes that he's going to be an astronaut when he grows up, Morgan couldn't imagine how to go from fantasy to reality. This is an unbridgeable gulf for the childhood mind—he can only fantasize about growing up. As Morgan talked about these things he started to feel "small, childish, unprepared, foolish."

He was able to identify the problem and tell me, "I don't want to do everything for my parents." But for a while he couldn't move forward: "Now I don't know what to do. I feel stuck." He felt he should be doing adult things—making plans, making money, getting "into" something—but he couldn't actually see himself taking these steps. They held no appeal whatsoever. They were simply things he ought to do. Things he should do. He saw these steps mapped out before him—school, university, job, house. While acknowledging the inherent wisdom of these goals, Morgan couldn't emotionally buy into them. On the contrary, when he thought about them, these steps took on an inescapable and oppressive quality, a weighty sense of expectation surrounding all the things he should do.

He called this feeling "the looming conveyor belt of life."

Morgan was caught between the powerful feeling of not wanting to get on the conveyor belt of life and the belief that he had no other choice. I was immediately struck by this metaphor, and since then I've met a number of young people in similar situations. When I refer to the conveyer belt image, it never fails to resonate with them.

Although he had classic adolescent issues, Morgan had a greater ability to reflect and own things than most teenagers.

Chronologically, of course, he was no longer a teenager. He was a young adult confronting a long-standing adolescent problem, so he could put into words what many adolescents feel but either can't articulate or admit. This is also why he was able to work in therapy so quickly. Most parents want their kids to be off and moving on their own in the world long before they hit their twenties, so it is a cautionary tale. But the good news is: even when you get it wrong the first time, you can get it right, more quickly, the second. '

"Will This Be on the Exam?"

Before a recent talk to parents at a girls' private school, I asked the principal what her biggest concern was. "The girls who can't tolerate making mistakes," she said. "The girls who are so anxious that they have to get everything right all the time. All of us—especially children—need to be free to make mistakes and learn from them."

School is one area where I see a marked difference between boys and girls. A friend who teaches in a university sees the results a few years after high school. It's not just that the young women greatly outnumber the young men, it's their attitudes. He's as impressed with the bright, hardworking and committed women as he is frustrated with the directionless, slacker boys that he just can't seem to motivate. The women study and worry about high marks, and the men party and worry about high scores on their favorite video games. While he's quick to point out that he sees plenty of exceptions—slacker females and high-achieving males—he wonders if we're raising a generation of guys who won't be prepared to do much of anything but watch their powerful wives go out and conquer the world.

My friend is only half-joking, but he also worries about the women he teaches because they seem so afraid to fail that he wonders if they're really engaging with the material. And let's face it, anyone afraid to fail and afraid to take risks is on one gloomy conveyor belt. This conveyor may be a little different from the one that boys like Morgan fear, but no more healthy or appealing.

Another friend recently told me a revealing story about the response he received to what he thought was a rather compelling lecture he'd given on an indigenous population in South America. An anthropology professor, he'd personally studied and visited the people and he knew a lot about their lives and culture and he presented what he knew with his usual passion—and showed his own photographs. He thought he'd rocked it. When he paused for questions and comments, though, the first thing he heard was a young woman asking: "Will this be on the exam?"

I'm sure every professor has heard this question at one time or another and what it reveals is that these students—who are in university after all and are presumably studying subjects that interest them—aren't engaging with the material. That's not the fault of the professors; it's the result of a system that is focused increasingly on marks (the "measurable outcome") and less on providing children and teenagers with the optimal spaces and opportunities for their intellectual and emotional growth. The is-this-going–to-be-on-the-exam question comes from a mind still primarily in the please-and-appease mode: just tell me what I need to know to make you happy. It has the fingerprints of all the overly involved helicopter and helicopter-lite adults who have herded and shepherded these young people up to this point.

School is the most common area for parental over-involvement, especially among the educated, high-achieving set. And it doesn't help that schools increasingly send the message that parents are responsible for their children's academic success. As parents, our prime objective should be to help our children develop their own positive relationship with academic achievement.

There are three unwelcome results when students don't develop this crucial relationship. First, it leads to student disengagement and often means Mom or Dad does too much of the schoolwork and almost all of the worrying. Second, the whole notion of school and achievement seems like such a burden that gaining skills and seeking jobs loses its natural appeal; this is the "looming conveyor belt of life" syndrome. It makes competing in the game of life "un-fun." Third, these kids become passive, authority-pleasing students, the kind who ask, "Will this be on the exam?"

Trusting Teachers

In the first world, the original world of the family, everything depends on Mom and Dad. If a kid's parents are happy, life is good. The situation turns sour only when the parents are mad or disappointed. The first world operates according to a guilt economy in the sense that in the child's mind, "bad" behavior and poor outcomes are linked to Mom and Dad's disapproval or disappointment, and the guilty or even shameful feelings this creates. When we fail, we feel we've been bad. Guilt is not a great motivator. In fact, when we feel guilty and ashamed, the strongest wish is often to withdraw and hide.

The second world is the big world outside of the family (what I often refer to as "reality"). At some point, children need to worry about their report card on their own behalf, something Morgan still wasn't doing in university. Moving from the first to the second world involves a transition from a guilt and shame economy to an anxiety economy. Literally, we need kids to become anxious on their own behalf. Unlike the first world, where we feel bad when we make mistakes, in this second world, where we must become aware of the dangers ahead, anxiety motivates us (ideally) to take appropriate action.

In our modern highly organized society, we require a moderate but fairly steady state of anxiety to be successful. We live in a future-oriented world: you must plan ahead (school to job to retirement, putting away taxes, anticipating deadlines) and anxiety is always future oriented. It is based on an anticipation of threat in the future that can be dealt with by action now. It is essential to planning, and dealing with the real world.

The trouble with anxiety is that it needs to be in the right amount. Too many young people struggle with anxiety. There are two kinds of anxiety problems we need to worry about with our kids—either too much or too little. Let's call the first one the female version, since it seems to show up more in girls than in boys (though there are certainly exceptions, both ways). Here the problem is too much anxiety and educators are struggling more than ever with students who are so anxious about their results that it interferes with performance and even creates physical health issues. In some students, the need for the highest marks can lead to a stifling perfectionism that results in growing piles of incomplete work. Or whose high stress level turns into a panic attack as they're sitting an exam, causing them to shut down and stop functioning at all. Even in the best of cases, this orientation promotes "is this going to be on the exam?" thinking.

The alternative to this pressure-cooker approach is for kids to avoid all this stress and angst by finding ways to distract themselves from the problems of the world: to disengage, relax, chill out and ideally feel no anxiety at all. Let's call this the male version. At its most extreme, this lack of direction leads to a loss of meaning in the world and the dark nihilism and empty hedonism of Kurt Cobain's chilling lyrics in Nirvana's anthemic song, "Smells Like Teen Spirit." The chorus of that song—"Here we are now, entertain us"—captures the sense of entitlement and indolence, while the verses depict a disengaged attitude toward the larger world of human endeavor, preferring the pleasant but utterly passive activity of hanging with friends in the basement.

In our society, we're lost if we don't have a certain level of stress about the future. It's stress that leads us to plan ahead, both short term and long. And that's precisely what Morgan wasn't doing.

To build the bridge to the second world, parents must foster the right kind of relationship with external authorities such as teachers and principals. As much as I complain about schools forcing parents into the counter-productive role of homework cop, I have a great deal of respect for teachers and the absolutely crucial job they do. Most of them do it well—and for a lot less money than they're worth. That's why I have three essential rules for talking with teachers:

1. Entrust: Tell them you appreciate and trust them.

2. Inform: Tell them you are trying to step back from policing homework and your child's academic life in general.

3. Empower: Tell them you see them as a vital authority in your child's life. Leave them feeling they have the authority to use both positive and negative (including reprimanding, failing, benching) reinforcement.

This sounds easy enough. But too often obligated parents act out of guilty responsibility, angry protectiveness or a sense of ownership of the disciplining function (or all three). A principal recently told me that when she suspends a boy—for fighting and injuring another boy, say, or for drinking on school property—the parents almost always ask: "How many other kids will find out he's been suspended?" Or: "He told the truth, isn't that one of your school's virtues? Then why suspend him?"

Clearly, these parents aren't sitting gratefully back on the bench. What's getting in their way? The usual: anxiety about their children's failures and over-identification with their successes. But there's another factor now too: when parents don't trust the school enough to leave the child in its capable hands, there are going to be problems.

Please and Appease

Several years earlier, when Morgan was still at a small private coed high school, his parents, Carol and Richard, had come to me for some guidance on how to handle him. They were the typical obligated parents with Carol, in particular, doing a great deal of active guidance. She was on top of the kids regarding school. "I check in with them every day when they come home: 'How was school? What's the homework?'" she told me. "This has become a daily monologue but I get short answers and a lot of avoidance."

Meanwhile, Morgan was just keeping his head above water at school, doing the absolute minimum. At this midway point in high school, he was not oriented to reality at all. His focus and concern about school, when it was there at all, was entirely on his parents. He was in first-world thinking. And for his parents, trying to reason with him was exasperating. The more they tried to point out the obvious to him, the more oblivious he became.

Carol described the 16-year-old as "honest to a fault," but his father believed trust was an issue because they'd caught him lying about school. The family was settling into a pattern: Carol and Richard would receive an e-mail from a teacher, then confront Morgan, who would admit to a "horrible, sick feeling" about screwing up. He didn't fight with his parents and was never belligerent; he didn't even put up a fight when his parents grounded him. Instead, he was crestfallen that he had disappointed them.

The family dynamic developing over school was not a good one. As Carol and Richard became more responsible and active, Morgan became increasingly passive and agreeable. The parents were gentle people, caring and concerned, and they encouraged Morgan and worried about him. They tried to reassure themselves that things would work out for him, but would then learn of another poor result or another assignment he hadn't handed in. This would upset them and lead them to address the problem with Morgan, sometimes in gentle, searching conversations, sometimes in angry confrontations.

For Morgan, these failures were painful for one reason—they created strife and unhappiness at home. He wasn't actually rude and defiant—on the contrary, he was a good boy who hated to upset his mom and dad, and avoiding their disappointment was his one clear motivation. The worst thing that could happen in his world—perhaps the only bad thing—was upsetting his parents. So he did what he had to do to please and appease his parents, just trying not to get caught most of the time, trying to "get away with it."

To make matters worse, Morgan was smoking marijuana. His mother and father knew well and actually quite liked his small close group of friends, a mix of girls and boys. When the gang visited, which was often, the kids were polite and engaging, and Carol and Richard could see how good they were to each other. But they were also aware that the group regularly smoked weed together—not during the school days as far as they could see, but sometimes after school and always on weekends.

The parents knew from their own teenage and university years that pot can be an ambition killer. Although they knew many cases, including their own, where recreational drugs (and drinking) had not interfered, they certainly knew cases where it had, including a close friend of Richard's, the infamous Jerry, who now had a quite marginal existence (in his 40s), and whom Richard and Carol and their community often had to support or even rescue. Jerry had even lived in their family home for a period, until Richard had to kick him out because the kids came home and found him passed out on the kitchen floor.

The question was: which path was Morgan on? His lack of effort at school and his generally nonengaged approach to the big world out there made them fear the worst. They knew the weed wasn't helping. But they felt hopeless because nothing they tried ever worked. When they got active and intervened, Morgan denied or lied or, if he was finally caught, showed that he felt distraught and guilty over the disappointment he'd caused his parents (the "horrible, sick feeling"). Then he would be on his best behavior for the next week or so. Inevitably, though—and this happened more quickly all the time—he would slip back into his old ways, and the pattern of denial and avoidance would begin again.

But then, if they stepped back, he seemed headed down the road to Jerry-ville, making bad decisions.

At the time, I hadn't developed my three rules for teaming up with teachers, so I didn't know to give Richard and Carol that advice. I wish I had: Morgan was disposed to be agreeable—he liked to please—and what they needed was a school, or more precisely some staff within the school (teacher, guidance counselor, vice-principal) who felt authorized to take a personal interest in Morgan, and turn the heat up on him at school, so that his parents could back off at home. He would have responded well, I believe. Unfortunately, turning the heat up was the one thing the school was not doing.

When Morgan failed a test, for example, the teacher didn't fail him, because school policy was that if you didn't pass a test, you would retake it. So his parents felt they had no choice but to ground him, even though they knew the consequences of failing a test should be a failing grade, not getting grounded. Later, when Morgan returned to my office as a young adult, he often reviewed his school years, especially between the fourth and eighth grades. It was somewhere in there, he figured, that he'd lost his way. In the sixth grade, he recalled, he didn't hand in an assignment and was in a panic about it. That he didn't get into trouble, and "got away with it," was a dangerous precedent. He gradually slid into a strategy of avoidance.

In one of our first sessions together, Carol and Richard described how Morgan had recently reported failing a test in the tenth grade. He'd been visibly upset and insisted that he thought he'd studied enough for the test and was disgusted with the result. He was mad at everyone. Mom's response was to tell him that this showed he needed a tutor, but that just led to a fight.

That failed test, I suggested, was just the kind of painful, non-catastrophic failure they should be cheering for. They should notice that it hurts: he's mad, upset, disgusted. This means he'll still learn if they stay out of his way and be supportive, compassionate bystanders. They should also note a few other things. First, he doesn't yet hold himself entirely accountable—he's mad at everyone else—and the child inside him wants to blame his parents. Second, Mom's push for a tutor took Morgan's eyes off his mistake and back on his parents. Third, notice the story-of-woe moment here, for example when he talks about "how he thought he'd studied enough." Listen, but don't be too gratifying: he's having this conversation partly to bring his anxiety down, but we want him to stay anxious—bearably anxious. Not overwhelmed, but anxious: because he should be.

I heard nothing from Carol and Richard until Morgan dropped out of university. In the meantime, though, I met plenty of other parents with similar struggles.

Don't Be a Homework Cop

Donny was driving his father crazy—and, worse, really stressing out his mother. Bruce and Amelia's two older kids were high achievers, first in high school and now in university, but number three didn't seem to care about anything but partying and having a good time. The 16-year-old's marks were dismal and he was completely irresponsible. After having reluctantly lent his son his beloved mountain bike, Bruce took his bike out for a ride and noticed that the bell had been sheared off. He was angry about the bell, of course, but also furious that Donny hadn't even bothered to mention it, let alone offered to replace it.

Bruce wasn't a client of mine, but I met him at a dinner party where, inevitably, the subject of parenting came up. I could tell Bruce was listening intently as I explained my approach. But I didn't know that he'd tried stepping back until I ran into him a few months later. That's when he told me about what he called, "My $1,500 experiment."

Donny had surprised him by saying he wanted to do a summer school course in chemistry. His son's desire for a slacker course-load the following school year wasn't perhaps the noblest motivation, and he was worried that his son would dog it and perhaps not even pass. The course was at a private school and cost $1,500, but Bruce convinced a skeptical Amelia. They would let the boy take the course, but stay scrupulously uninvolved. As Bruce said, "What have we got to lose—well, except the money?"

He resolved to wake Donny every morning, but not to hound him about getting out of bed. Nor would he nag his son about attendance, studying or marks. He would stop being a home-work cop and just be a dad. If the kid was ready on time, Bruce dropped him off at school, but that was it. Well, except for one comment he couldn't help but make: as they drove to school one morning they passed a lineup outside an employment office and Bruce cracked, "That's plan B, Donny."

Other than that, Bruce stuck to his plan A. When Donny scored 27 percent on the first week's test, his dad said and did nothing. Week two's mark was 54. But the final three weeks were all between 70 and 80 and, since lab work also factored into the final grade, the boy ended up with 74 percent. Not genius level or anything, but not an embarrassment either. And while Bruce knew this "success" didn't mean Donny had com-pletely grown up, he was going to try to never be a homework cop again. "I'm a convert," he told me.

Unlike Bruce, Morgan's parents weren't able to use my advice the first time around. In fact, they were with me much as Morgan was with them: unable to take advice and put it into action. I wasn't surprised, given today's over-parenting culture. Carol and Richard were caught in a system that increasingly puts the role of the "heavy" onto the parents—just where we don't want it.

We need external authority to work its magic on our kids. But, these days, parents too often end up being the ones who must deliver the painful blow, the so-called natural consequence for a child's error.

Well-meaning policies developed by schools—or at the board level or even in the Ministry of Education—often do more harm than good. "No Student Fails" policies mean there's not enough "reality" in the system. And I've had to talk princi-pals into failing children. "Agenda books" to spy on kids take the responsibility off the students and put it on the parents. Tool kits and similar initiatives to "engage" parents can instead encourage parents to intervene and interfere in all the worst ways. Yes, research shows that parental involvement in kids' school can be good—if it's the right kind of involvement. And policing is the wrong kind.

Naturally, we all want to help keep our kids on track, but we also want them to develop their own relationship with academics and achievement, to gain a personal sense of responsibility. Supporting your kids in school is a tightrope walk: you have to help and support them enough that they don't get discouraged or even give up. But if you give too much, they learn to lean on your support, guidance and direction. And what you get is learned helplessness. So when you err on this tightrope, you must err on both sides—sometimes you have to err on the side of neglect.

If we work too hard to keep our kids on track at school, if we accept too much responsibility for their success, we naturally interfere with their developing capacity to take things on for themselves. This is when we can easily become homework cops—or a "keeper of the nag," as one mom described her role to me. But a vicious cycle develops: the more mom nags and cheerleads, the more kid tunes out; the more kid tunes out, the more mom nags and cheerleads. And so on.

The problem is that many parents work harder than their children at school. But instead of worrying about A's and B's, our first order of business should be to help students grow up emotionally and become more responsible for themselves. So more parental control—setting and policing a work schedule in high school, for example—can actually be counter-productive because it confirms for teenagers that school is something they do to please Mom and Dad, and where they do the minimum necessary to keep the parental units off their back. Instead, parents often need to back off from scheduling and organizing, and give their kids some time and space to learn for themselves how to deal with the demands of school.

Backing off almost always means results will have to get worse before they get better. But children learn from mistakes; we all do. Not studying leads to poor marks and even failing grades; misbehaving leads to punishment (detentions, loss of privileges, loss of status). These things hurt teenagers and they don't like them. And as long as we don't finger-wag and say, "I told you so"—which only draws their attention back to us—they learn to respect this painful aspect of reality. Instead, be there for them sympathetically, just like you were when they scraped their knee in the playground.

Finding Flow

Morgan's parents couldn't walk the tightrope. Unable or unwilling to let go of her role, Carol monitored Morgan's homework, kept "supporting" him, and eventually even went online to register him in his first-year university courses, most of which she'd chosen for him. She wasn't just holding the worry ball, she owned it. Morgan, meanwhile, stayed locked in the first world, the guilt economy. As he put it himself, he went to university "for his parents."

When parents take on this level of ownership of the problem there is actually no good outcome possible. The response is either an angry, defiant rejection of good advice or a passive, directionless, guilty kid who is disposed to like and be liked and to be a "good boy" (which sounds good, except that upon reaching young adulthood he has no idea how to take on the world for himself).

Carol's good, honest intentions and her "mother-worry" were obvious to Morgan. And he felt, on some level that was hard to acknowledge, terribly sad about it. By the time he came to me, he was well aware that his parents had reasonable hopes and expectations for him, just as he knew that they had parented him with patience, love and generosity. And this made him feel guilty and ashamed. He realized he should have motivations and goals, but this awareness left him cold; the more he realized it was something he ought to do, the more it was robbed of its appeal, the more it became the looming conveyor belt of life.

One day I asked Morgan to tell me more about this metaphor. "Everybody has a dream, but they lose it to reality, they get a job because they have to," he explained. "I see people who end up being something they don't want to be. They're 50 and they don't like their life." And yet, he went on to say, he felt disillusioned that he didn't even have any dream in particular. He never saw the point of high school and the whole career, marriage and kids thing didn't appeal to him in the slightest. It all seemed planned out, but he wanted to break out of it somehow. "I have no purpose," he admitted. "Why aren't I fantasizing about the future? I have a nagging feeling that there should be something more productive that I should be doing. But why produce?"

He felt bleak as he realized his situation. In the absence of his parents' agenda, he was at a loss as to what was on his agenda. Finally having established freedom (from his parents) he was lost on what to do with it. And, as Morgan noted, "I've never been that committed to a plan."

Most of the time, up to now, Morgan had lived—or at least tried to live—anxiety-free. "I don't ever feel anxious, nervous," he admitted. "I've felt it, but I can't remember when. Since I've been back, nothing's been bothering me much." He thought for a bit and then said, "I tell myself there's nothing to worry about just as long as I don't die."

But as he went on, the more it became clear that he had painful moments when this strategy broke down and he was flooded with panic. Sometimes, late at night, it slipped past his guard and he started to think about the future. Occasionally, it struck in unexpected moments when he was around others and was suddenly reminded of his own situation because his friends were going back to school. Or he'd read something that reminded him of what he had studied in university and what he had given up. He had sudden "panic sweats" as a feeling of paralyzing dread came over him. And so he had worked harder to avoid going there in his mind.

From Morgan's perspective, his choices were grim: sign up for the conveyor belt and live a stressful, onerous life, or stay off it and endure endless ennui. What is appealing here? Nothing.

He lacked pleasurable engagement with the world, he realized, not just with his studies but with everything the world has to offer. When he was in high school, Morgan fiddled around with the guitar and at one point enjoyed jamming with friends. "I don't jam anymore," Morgan realized, meaning both musically and more generally. He lacked a fulfilling and creative engagement with reality.

He lacked flow.

A widely used concept in psychology and counseling for the last couple of decades, "flow" means focused motivation. Crucial for both productivity and overall happiness, it refers to those moments when a person is fully immersed in an activity, emotionally focused, creatively involved in something that provides a feeling of mastery and competence. In sports, we talk about "getting our head in the game" or being "in the zone" and that's what flow is. Flow is what puts the play into work and it's the closest scientists have come to defining what gives life meaning. Obstacles to flow include too much anxiety (too much worry about outcome, too much self-consciousness) and boredom (withdrawal from the world and following, often unconsciously, a safe, risk-averse approach). Any kid who feels the conveyor belt is looming lacks flow.

As we have seen, in the right amounts, anxiety is a powerful motivator. A precursor to "arousal," anxiety is essential for flow. When someone is in a state of arousal, important brain functions kick in, creating a state of alertness and a "readiness to respond." So it was completely predictable that the flow-less Morgan would declare: "I'm bored."

Safe but dull, boredom is one of the inescapable consequences of avoidance. But boredom is also the pain—the burnt hand, as it were—that can motivate someone in Morgan's position to learn and change.

"Yes," I replied, "and when you're not bored you're in a panic. It's either one or the other and that's not a very good system."

And so we went on a quest for flow.

Minding the Children

When I met them the first time around, Carol and Richard had a level of involvement in Morgan's academic life that was not particularly out of the ordinary. They are certainly not the only parents to have overseen homework on a daily basis—in fact, this is something the majority of parents do these days. They are not the only parents who've become angry with a child for not attending to his responsibilities, who alternately threatened and encouraged him to get to work, who lectured him on the logic of his actions (or lack thereof) and who regularly provided him with advice and feedback about his performance. And who let him know how disappointed they were with his results.

But imagine if we conducted ourselves this way in the playground, if we kept such a close eye on the productivity or thoughtfulness of our child's engagement with the park and its inhabitants. If we considered our role there to include teaching, encouraging, cheering and redirecting; if we did that each time our child erred in the park—tripped while running, gave up in a game of tag, went the wrong way up the slide, aimlessly sifted sand through his fingers instead of "building something"—the park would stop being such a fun place, that's for sure.

"That's all fine and dandy," parents say to me, "but kids like playing in the park, so it's easy to sit back on the park bench. They hate school, so there we have no choice but to push."

Wrong. But this belief can easily become a self-fulfilling prophecy. Convinced that kids won't care about school results unless they make them care, many parents act accordingly, thus sending the message to their kids that this is the way things work. Although they are certainly not intending to send this message, their actions indicate to the child that it's normal (and expected) to hate school and to resist doing work, or to try to get away with doing as little as possible.

It's not true, though: children don't always hate school, they sometimes even like it. And parents are not required to force kids to attend to school in order for them to learn to care about it and put in a good effort there. In fact, school is an excellent place for finding "flow"—whether in the classroom, on sports teams or in the drama club, school provides children with an incredible "playground" of resources, challenges and organized activities.

Remember: children are not missing that part of their brain that allows them to be anxious on their own behalf. Those capacities are there and ready to kick in; the only thing that can interfere with this are Mom and Dad finger-wagging and continuing to take on the worrying for their kids. It doesn't

. matter if it's a reasonable message—"put in a good effort"—it's still parental pressure.

Just as in the park, parents need to be there for their children, taking an active interest and pleasure in their efforts. This was part of the problem for Morgan: he needed his parents to witness and validate his interests, but he had got to a point where any parental interest in his life felt oppressive and deflating. When Morgan started thinking about heading out West, this tension came to a head. He liked the idea of finding a job at a ski resort and he knew some people in Whistler. But he worried about telling his parents of his plan. He feared they'd object to the idea, of course, but he was just as apprehensive that even if they agreed to it, they would become over-involved.

Worse, Morgan realized that even if his parents did none of these things, he'd still get hung up over what he thought they were thinking. We called these his internalized parents. Making this distinction was helpful for Morgan. He saw these "people," not his external parents, as his real problem. It was these internalized parents, he realized, that more than anything interfered with his quest for flow. Meanwhile, Carol and Richard worked at keeping their old expectations and their fears out of the way, especially since Morgan was now 20. They agreed they had to rein in their own feelings about the situation in order to project what Morgan needed most from them: a calm sense of assurance that he would do fine, that he would work it out. They had learned how unhelpful their own all-too-evident anxiety about Morgan was: it only made everything more dire and upsetting for him. What they had to do was shift perspective, so that they could see their son from an angle that was not so limited by their own hopes and fears.

When parents look only for what they expect to see or fear will happen, it is hard for them to see anything else. Most of the time we are unaware of how deeply our personal expectations influence what we see and how we interpret it. Morgan's interests in British Columbia were tied to skiing and snowboarding, but also a burgeoning interest in the outdoors. Yet these interests and their value to Morgan (for example, as places to find flow) had escaped his parents up to that point. His trips out of town they had associated with escapism and partying (and, of course, those accounted for at least some of Morgan's interest). Seeing other aspects of their son required them to step out of the mental straitjacket of their own hopes and fears.

I often find myself pointing out to parents: you won't notice what you need to see if you're not looking. Minding our children requires altering our expectations. It means reminding ourselves that the only way we can see what we didn't already know about our children—a hidden talent, say, or a new interest—is to step outside of our own assumptions. If we look only for what we expect to see, that's all we'll ever see, but if we watch carefully, we'll see things in our kids that we've never seen before.

So when Morgan began to talk about Whistler and the opportunities for employment there, Carol and Richard sat on that bench as best they could. Although they nodded in understanding and waited to see what Morgan wanted to do, it was tough for them. But it always is: despite how simple it sounds, minding our children is hard.

As his external parents put themselves back on the park bench, Morgan began to liberate himself from his internal parents, and this meant he started to size up reality for himself, really for the first time. Few of his friends were still around town—most of his gang from high school had successfully moved on and were doing well at university. Increasingly, hanging out with those who were still around town lost its appeal—there wasn't much new to be found there anymore. And, increasingly, that whole chilling, hanging in the basement, smoking weed, playing video games thing appeared like a bad idea to him.

A good-looking guy, Morgan had always enjoyed being relatively strong and athletic. Now he took a look at his level of fitness and was unimpressed. He began to work out, and got into walking. Actually walking and thinking, a pattern that started after our sessions because he would walk home (a good hour) afterward.

Smoking weed took on another perspective too. He started to notice how weed affected his fitness, his sleep, even his ability to enjoy things. This was an epiphany he reported to me after one of his long walks: when he was smoking a lot of weed he was actually less happy overall.

And as I watched his parents do their best, I saw how Morgan changed. The anxiety faded, replaced by excitement and even confidence. He wasn't running away to Whistler; in fact, he'd was making plans for what he'd do the following year. He'd contacted a couple of universities about re-admission and looked into improving his high-school marks because he was thinking he might like to try business school eventually. He'd renewed contact with a family friend now living in the West who was involved in green technologies, something Morgan increasingly thought was "cool." He'd also developed a good workout routine, something he definitely didn't have when I first met him.

At our last meeting, he told me he had a one-way ticket, but had also applied to some schools for when he returned. "I need to work on trusting my own judgment," he said. "I know now that doubt leads to procrastination." I remember it as a wonderful moment. I knew just how good it felt to him to make this decision, to successfully become his own boss, to accept the doubt and uncertainty, to take mature actions by applying to schools—to grab the worry ball from his parents.

He left for Whistler the next week.

DO talk about school and education

Obviously, you want to show a respect for education, but you want to do so by projecting a belief that your child will, step-by-step, engage in school on his own. Try not to respond literally to common early-childhood complaints, such as "I hate school" and "It's so boring," by trying to talk your child into liking or committing to school (by, say, explaining—yet again—the advantages and importance of education). Instead, be sympathetic to the general message ("I find reality to be difficult and not always fun"), and curious to hear what's going on. It's good to talk about learning and education, but it's not always easy. Parents often ask me to provide examples of questions that they can ask to get their kids to talk about their day and their experiences at school because the old "How was school?" often doesn't get much of a response. I don't have any magic questions, and don't believe there are any. It's all about the roles in the conversation: often it doesn't matter what specific question you ask, it's where you're coming from—or where your child thinks you're coming from—that matters. Often the fact that you're asking at all seems to feel intrusive and unwelcome to children, particularly teenagers. So be available, be interested. And if your opening query doesn't open anything up, be patient and see what he or she comes up with to talk about.

In the end, the key to talking with your kids about school and achievement is listening. Try to listen without an agenda. You won't always succeed, but you should always try. If you show an interest, a genuine interest free from your own agendas, he or she will begin to talk, but be prepared to hear stories off the topics you're most interested in (an amusing class clown, what happened during the fire alarm). Just enjoy the stories; don't offer editorials and judgments. When your children experience you as nonjudgmental (or at least relatively nonjudgmental: you'll react when it's important) they will see you as someone helpful to come to, as opposed to please-and-appease. When it comes to their school experience, don't direct, just listen. Don't buy into the mistaken notion that kids need to be pushed to be interested in school. Pushing isn't required; your interest is.

DON'T assume personal responsibility for your child's academic effort

These days, this is really hard to do. The social messaging that you must not fail your children at school is so strong and consistent that it takes a deliberate effort to stay immune to the madness. Unfortunately, schools often unwittingly play into it. For example, they will simplistically tell parents that "being involved" in their children's academic lives is good for their academic futures, without saying how to be involved. It is good to be involved by forming strong, positive relationships with teachers, taking an active interest in the school and the school community, and demonstrating a respect for education and learning. But initiatives such as log books for parents to monitor and review homework involve them in ways that aren't beneficial for developing a good long-term attitude toward school and learning. All children need teachers and parents to play this organizing role in the first years, and some children—for example, those with certain learning disabilities—will need this extra organizational support for some time. But all kids need to learn that school is their concern, and most kids are capable of learning this far earlier than our current system is designed for. Make it your priority as a parent to help your kids develop their own relationship with school and achievement.

DO build alliances with external authority

Teachers, coaches and camp counselors teach our kids about reality. They set limits and give essential feedback about the consequences of actions: "When I don't put in a good effort, I get a disappointing result; when I stop working hard in practice and games on my competitive sports team, my coach lets me know he expects more from me." When this doesn't happen, some essential learning fails to occur. In order for our children to engage with the world out there in a creative and productive manner, we need these people to play positive, authoritative roles in their lives. This often requires a specific effort because external authorities are increasingly caught between demanding or critical parents and strict regulations and policies. So follow this three-step plan: entrust (say you appreciate and trust them); inform (explain that you are no longer going to be the "homework cop"—or any other kind of "cop"); and empower (assure them that they are a vital authority in your child's life). Sending this message of trust and appreciation gives the important people in our kids' lives the confidence they need to act authoritatively, using both carrot and stick to motivate. By empowering them to act authoritatively with your child, you send a "better coming from you than me" message.

DO go for flow

It's not top grades your child needs to get at school, especially between kindergarton and the tenth grade. It's flow. So if they are getting average marks in the fourth grade, but really getting into sports teams, or the band, or organizing things, then notice this—your interest will be immensely supportive to your child, who will experience you as a real fan—someone who believes in them and finds their interests and talents to be cool. The jungle gym–climbing kid is in a flow state—and the park bench (present but not controlling; separate but interested) is the best place for parents in order to make that kind of flow happen.

Five

Sex, Drugs and Video Games

Jamie was the hockey player every coach loved. An excellent playmaker, he was also responsible defensively so his coaches sent him out to lead the power play and to kill penalties. The 16-year-old was a leader off the ice as well; his teammates looked up to him, listened to him and relied on him, especially since he was the guy who played even better in big games and when the score was close. He wasn't just the best player on the team, he was a natural team captain.

His parents—especially his dad, Arthur—were proud of him, of course, and loved watching him play. They were also happy that he wasn't just a jock; he was a reasonably strong student and was affectionate and helpful toward his two younger sisters, who adored him. The family lived in an affluent neighborhood and the kids socialized well, tended to be liked by their teachers and generally succeeded out there in the world. Arthur and Giselle agreed that none of their kids were particularly strong in the respect department: they tended to do the absolute minimum around the house, often "forgot about" what they were asked to do and generally found ways to get their focused, organized parents to do things for them. But for the most part, the family functioned relatively smoothly.

Until Jamie discovered weed. In the tenth grade, he and his friends started to smoke pot together on the weekends, playing video games and "chilling." Giselle had experimented with pot when she was younger and Arthur smoked throughout his university years and still did occasionally in social situations. So when they learned that Jamie was getting high, they were concerned but not too freaked out. Their position was, "As long as he keeps his act together at school, we're okay with it." Their initial position, that is.

Figuring out how to respond to a kid's growing interest in the "bad" things out there—sex and drugs and rock 'n' roll—has changed in important ways in the last few decades. In the 1950s and '60s, maybe even into the '70s, rock 'n' roll represented a potentially dangerous counter-cultural attitude. It threatened older people who could not relate to it, and who tried to limit teenagers' access to it. (Elvis Presley's gyrating hips were initially a scandal, and when the Rolling Stones appeared on *The Ed Sullivan Show* in 1967, they had to change the lyrics of "Let's Spend the Night Together" to "let's spend some time together.") Today, many parents—who, of course, grew up listening to rock—enjoy much of the same music their kids do.

So while gangsta rap held no appeal to Arthur and Giselle, and the charms of Simon & Garfunkel were lost on Jamie, there were songs they all enjoyed, and sometimes the family minivan was pumping as the family rolled down the highway rocking out to Pink Floyd's "The Wall," yelling at the teacher to "Leave those kids alone!"

Though music may no longer be an intergenerational sore spot, contemporary parents have found other cultural issues to fret about. They can be torn between a wish to be liberal and understanding (and, in many cases, not a hypocrite) and yet still feel a need to be protective. As Jamie's interest in pot grew, so did his parents' concern. And as people who knew the score, Arthur and Giselle could not remain as blissfully unaware as their parents had been. Giselle found a bong in Jamie's cupboard and Arthur noticed that he would go "to the park" with his friends and when he returned, 10 minutes later, scurry down to the basement. What would this habit do to his development as a student? As a person? Fortunately, Jamie's school performance didn't seem too badly affected. While some kids start smoking marijuana during the school day, Jamie restricted his use to after school and weekends. But it did have a negative effect on his hockey.

When Jamie started to get high before games and practices, it ushered in unfamiliar conflict to the family. Since Arthur had no problems identifying when his son was high, he'd lose it when Jamie climbed into the car with bloodshot eyes and reeking of weed. "What are you doing?" he'd bellow. "You can't play hockey like that! Don't you realize you're letting your team down?" Man, I could relate: if watching my son merely cough up the puck is painful, I could only imagine what Arthur was going through.

And let his team down is exactly what Jamie started to do. Once the best player on his team, he soon wasn't even playing at the level required to compete in his league. When he came to the games high, he was lost on the ice, a complete non-factor. The deterioration in his play was screamingly obvious to all. For Arthur, it was excruciatingly painful. Watching his son sleepwalk around the ice was bad enough, but Arthur's sense of guilt that his son was letting down the team was even worse. Sitting in the stands, he felt humiliated and had a hard time making eye contact with the other parents. He dreaded Jamie's games.

Meanwhile, the conflict escalated at home. No longer restricted to the car when Jamie climbed in stoned, the family fights broke out at any time as Arthur and Giselle began to monitor and question Jamie about his drug use. When the parents resolved to "sit down" with their son and "have a talk" about the problem, things unraveled in seconds as Jamie quickly became defensive and unreasonable. The more his parents signaled their concern, the more Jamie was motivated to insist: "Get out of my face." Their concern actually seemed to make the problem worse: Jamie began to spend less time around the house and more time hanging out with his friends (with whom he would inevitably get high), and his clean and sober hockey appearances became rarer and rarer.

Arthur and Gisele were learning what many parents have learned at this stage: sometimes trying to exert your parental influence only makes matters worse. They were not making any inroads on the problem; instead, they had created new, unhappy problems with Jamie at home, and the teenager's irritation with his parents, and his overriding preoccupation with evading them and keeping them at bay, was completely overshadowing the problems on his hockey team—one of the things that he really needed to pay attention to.

When we play the gatekeeper role, we take our kids' attention off the real world and the actual consequences of their actions. Instead, we keep their focus on us and how they can avoid our disapproval and restrictions. Parental fear sets us up to be gatekeepers, especially with sex and drugs. But getting too busy with our parental anxiety (acting on our worries too often in prescriptive and restrictive ways) makes us the problem in our child's life—we become what he or she needs to worry about, not the real problems out there in the world we're desperately clamoring about.

The more Arthur yelled at Jamie about his obligations to his teammates, the less the boy seemed to think about them and the more oblivious he became. Where once he had been the quite selfless leader on his team, he now seemed grossly unconcerned with his responsibilities. His demeanor around the house deteriorated surprisingly quickly and negative energy crept in there. Arthur and Giselle became more exasperated with him than ever and tended to snap at him; he was surly and when he did get around to doing what he was being "nagged" about, he did the absolute minimum. His obvious lack of regard for putting in an effort seemed so brazen, Arthur and Giselle took it as an intentional "in your face."

Any parent would find it really hard to stand back at this point. Jamie's conduct felt like "an embarrassment to the whole family," as his father put it to me. And I could see how that was. It was hard not to sympathize: Jamie really was being an idiot and his parents were now at a loss about what to do. Intervening seemed to make it worse, and doing nothing felt worse than neglectful. They'd reached the point where they were considering withdrawing Jamie from hockey until his behavior and attitude changed, even though they knew that this would not only enrage him, but also likely alienate him further. They felt paralyzed. They were angry at Jamie, they worried about him, and felt defeated and guilty about their failure here. Arthur was having trouble focusing at work. And neither Arthur nor Giselle was sleeping well.

Doomed to Fail

Springing Jamie's parents out of the paralysis this predicament created required helping them understand why any pressure they put on Jamie was doomed to fail. One of the tasks of growing up is learning to take responsibility, to move from the first world, where we do things to please and appease our parents, to the second world, where we have our own goals to live up to. But parental efforts to ease this process are inherently paradoxical. "Helping a child help himself" is, at a certain level, impossible. As the old saying goes, "You can lead a horse to water, but you can't make him drink."

When parents provide their horse with a stream—a stream that is not only necessary for his survival but also offers all the opportunities that he might want for himself—and he still refuses to drink from it, they have to accept that there's nothing else they can do in the active or directive sense at this time. In fact, acting here, finding a way to force the horse to drink (threats) or induce the horse to drink (bribes) only exacerbates the problem. There are only two possible outcomes: either the child does what he's told, which might seem great for the immediate problem but is actually bad for the overall task of taking on responsibility (because now he's just being a "good boy"), or he does what's developmentally appropriate and says, "You're not the boss of me" and proceeds to do exactly the opposite of what you want him to do.

If your aim is to have your child assume more responsibility for himself in the world, then the best thing you can do is to ensure that you give him responsibility. And that means resisting the powerful impulse to take it on for him.

We had to put Arthur and Giselle back on the park bench, while still ensuring that Jamie was in a safe park. It had to be one where he could be hurt—even hurt painfully—but not catastrophically. I encouraged them to take an all-or-nothing approach in the outside world and, as long as the risks aren't in the catastrophic range, stand back. When a teenager wakes up with a hangover, don't finger-wag. Remember that the natural consequence of a person's stupid choice is its own teacher. Hangovers suck. In fact, if it's a particularly bad or enduring hangover, eventually you may even want to teach her your own hangover cure.

"Non-catastrophic" can mean pretty bad mistakes too, with attendant bad consequences—don't study all term and fail the course, break the behavior code too many times and get suspended. These things hurt, they really do. The only thing that can interfere with their instructive value is a finger-wagging parent.

But you must stay watchful for catastrophic failure. That's another part of minding our children—paying attention so you'll know if something really bad looms. Suicidal thoughts, of course. But also if a kid has avoided school so much that she can no longer bring herself to attend and has basically taken refuge in her room. Criminal charges, addiction (including computer addiction), pregnancy and sexual risk-taking, social ostracism—these are some of the big ones parents worry about. And we need to be watchful enough that we intervene before these catastrophic developments occur—to let our child learn from his or her mistakes up to the point where it is no longer safe. That's when we need to step in. Despite all our fears, though, these catastrophic failures rarely happen when parents are paying mindful attention.

I had Arthur and Giselle make a distinction between "inside the house" and "outside the house." Inside, be authoritative, in-control parents: insist your kids meet a clear and finite list of expectations. Outside, take the interested, supportive bystander position and avoid gatekeeping. As long as a catastrophic error isn't in the works, trust the power of the school of hard knocks to work its magic.

So when it came to Jamie's life outside the house (school, hockey, sex and drugs and rock 'n' roll), Arthur and Giselle stepped back to give him some time and space to work things out for himself. They certainly continued to pay close attention and to ensure that there was a "safety net" around him out there in the world. They made close contact with the external authorities in Jamie's life. They did this behind the scenes and without his knowledge. Think of this as ensuring the safety of the park by making sure the park attendants are aware of the situation.

Checking in with school, they learned that Jamie continued to more or less keep up with academic expectations. But the teachers had observed a change in his attitude. "Defiance" would be too strong a word as he was still primarily an agreeable lad, but certainly a lack of enthusiasm and perhaps body language and an overall style that was a bit less respectful than in the past. A bit "arrogant" was how one teacher described him.

Following the three rules from the last chapter, Arthur and Giselle let the teachers know how appreciative they were for their work with Jamie. Second, they let the school know they would be stepping back. They didn't give all the details—they decided not to tell the school about Jamie's pot use because that would have felt too much like "busting him." But they admitted that Jamie was giving a lot of push-back at home and they had decided to give him some space. Third, they empowered the teachers and principal to do what they thought best with Jamie. If he was being "too arrogant," they should feel free to respond in whatever way they thought was appropriate—they had the parents' support.

The hockey team, the family's sports "village," was where Jamie's behavior was most upsetting. So Arthur approached

Keith, the coach, with the same three-part message. First, he expressed how much he and Giselle appreciated his work with Jamie. Second, he explained that they were aware of the weed-smoking but had done as much as they could, short of pulling him off the team, and that they were going to step back and let the boy make his own choices. And, third, he told Keith: "Do what you will—carrot or stick. Don't hold back on our behalf."

The message here is: "He won't listen to us, but he's likely to listen to you." Not only is this probably true, but saying it, and now having the coach believe it, suddenly makes it more likely to become true.

Indeed, it worked. When Jamie arrived high to the next game, the coach allowed him to dress and take the warm-up, but then benched him for the entire game: three full periods of sitting there while his teammates slowly lost. It was excruciating, humiliating and enraging.

Jamie was furious in the car on the way home. Out of nowhere, he suddenly wanted to talk about hockey with Arthur. "Keith is an idiot!" he proclaimed. "Everyone hates him!"

When neither his mother nor father said anything and a silence filled the car for a bit, Jamie softened his stand. "Maybe one period," he conceded, "but three! I mean, What the hell? He's such a power-tripper!"

I had warned Arthur and Giselle about this Story of Woe moment. It's true Jamie was hurting but he was also trying to recruit his parents into a sympathetic position and to join him in blaming Keith. He didn't want to have to face the reality of why this had happened. But if they gratified him by respond-ing too sympathetically—helped him feel better by going along with him, or even engaging with him too much—they would have been helping him avoid the problem. They had to leave him with it.

The description of Keith as a power-tripper was a ludicrous misrepresentation of the facts, so Arthur really had to bite his tongue. Being too critical and condemnatory wasn't going to help either. That would just invite Jamie to shift his anger back to the parents, thereby leaving the second world altogether and regressing to the first. Realizing that less was more at this point, Arthur said nothing.

That just seemed to draw Jamie's anger anyway. "I knew it!" he raged at his parents. "I knew you'd take his side!"

They refused to take the bait and, over the next few days, noted that Jamie seemed more affectionate and even a bit needy. Giselle made him a batch of chocolate chip cookies and they had a nice time in the kitchen together while he ate a few. He didn't bring up the benching and neither did they. But they knew the message had made it through. Jamie never got high before a game again. From that point on, he only got high after the games.

Being "Bad"

I often tell that story when I give talks and when I get to the end, I add: "Good outcome!" That gets a laugh. I'm not joking, though. Given the range of possible outcomes at this point, this is actually quite a good one. Jamie learned that he cared enough about his teammates and coach that he was willing to change his habits. In fact, this is actually the kind of outcome we're looking for. Why? Because it's all about his relationship with the outside world and suddenly we can see him being concerned about the consequences of his actions: his standing among his peers, his coach's respect, the negative results of his drug use. This is exactly what we want him focused on.

Of course, from a parent's perspective, there is a better outcome—the boy stops smoking weed altogether. That's why my "good outcome" comment seems more like a punch line than a serious observation. In truth, this is not a laughing matter at all; but it is one many parents get wrong. When they do, they risk alienating their son and prolonging his wish to ignore the consequences of his actions and stay in the first world of emotional functioning.

Sex and drugs and rock 'n' roll, the infamous trinity of teenage evils that I have riffed on for the title of this chapter, have long aroused parents' moral anxieties. When I advise parents on how to deal with these types of issues, I often have to help them work through their utter moral condemnation of their child's actions, before we can get to a place where we can start to work on solutions. "It's just wrong," they say. "We can't accept this behavior." "That's a zero-tolerance thing." "It goes against our basic family values."

Fine, no problem. Values are important and if kids don't learn them from their parents, where are they going to get them? The question is: how best to lead your child to truly adopt and operate according to your family's values? This is a pragmatic question, and parents can easily get lost when they think along simplistic good versus bad moral lines. Left unchecked, this approach leads eventually and inevitably to parental ultimatums. The endgame here is the position espoused by the now thoroughly discredited "Tough Love." movement: "Either you stop doing X or you don't live in this house."

When you go there, there's no possibility of a solution, but it's where Amanda's parents, Aileen and Phil, were headed when I first met them. A 15–year-old in private school, the girl had thrived during the holidays at her summer camp, where she loved the outdoors and all the activities (such as windsurfing and wakeboarding) and the social world. Many of the campers had been going there for years and so they'd grown up together as a gang in the summers. Unlike Amanda's all-girl school, this was a coed environment, one she felt very comfortable in. After her first year of high school, she spent the entire two months at the camp, preparing to enter the counselor-in-training program the following year. She had a blast.

She also engaged in sexual exploration with a boy for the first time. During visitors' day, Aileen found out about it when she read a confidential letter lying on Amanda's bed. Amanda called it spying; Aileen called it an accident. Whatever it was, it ruined the next six months of their lives together. When Amanda returned from camp, the parents, under Aileen's direction, kept close tabs on her and required her to check in frequently. They had done their own investigating to figure out who the boy was, and what he and Amanda had done together. They forbade their daughter from going to his home, and they instigated a strict curfew, which inevitably led to ugly confrontations.

One Sunday afternoon, Amanda said she was going to meet a friend at Starbucks. Checking up on her a couple of hours later, Phil discovered she hadn't gone there and caught her coming out of the home of Toby, the boy she wasn't to see. When Phil ordered her home, there was a scene in front of neighbors. A terrible iciness had crept into a home that had been an extremely happy one: an only child, Amanda was pretty, athletic and eager to please. This first surprising sign of trouble hit all three of them hard.

I didn't know what to expect when I met Amanda, who turned out to be a thoughtful, quietly confident girl with a short, sporty haircut. She admitted she was there at her parents' request, but she didn't seem too put out about it. In fact, she was relieved to talk about her family, which had become a place of unhappy stress for her.

Beyond the grief it caused her parents, Amanda was okay with her choices around sexual exploration. Although she and Toby had not yet had intercourse, they had talked about it, and meanwhile had been engaging in occasional oral sex since the summer. For many young women, these first sexual explorations can involve troublesome power dynamics, particularly when it comes to oral sex, but this really didn't seem to be the case for Amanda. For one thing their activities were mutual as opposed to being focused exclusively on the male's wishes, and for another the two of them clearly had a relationship beyond the sexual one, that was positive and respectful. Also, they obviously spent lots of time together not fooling around.

From her descriptions, I could see Amanda was enjoying school and her social world; Toby went to a different school so they mostly saw each other on weekends. She was, in fact, doing well all around: an active, successful high-school student. The problem was at home. "They don't trust me as much," she lamented. "I want them to give me the benefit of the doubt."

She was all too aware of her parents' feelings and what she had "put them through." She cried as she told me how much she didn't want to hurt them. "I feel bad they're so shocked. They see it as abnormal." She felt terrible about the lying and hiding: "I tried to protect them from this."

When I met with the parents alone and asked them why they felt they needed to keep such a close eye on Amanda, to be so restrictive, their answer was clear and definitive. "It's just wrong," Aileen insisted. "A 15-year-old girl should not be having sex. She's too young. Full stop."

Phil supported Aileen's restrictiveness because of his parental fears: "I worry about her reputation. I think she's a pretty smart girl and can probably take care of herself with any guy, but I worry what other people will think. She's naïve that way, she doesn't understand how she might be judged."

And so they restricted and intervened, monitored, questioned and set limits. And the more they over-parented, the more distant child and parents became.

"Why doesn't she trust us?" asked Phil, referring to the fact that Amanda no longer listened to them, especially when it came to their advice about relationships and sex. Aileen categorized it frankly as a "catastrophe" and a "train wreck." But she was able to see how unproductive this was. "I slip into being critical. I really judge it negatively. I see her as . . ." She didn't say it, but I knew the word she was thinking of was "slutty."

Meanwhile, Phil's anxiety forced him to do something. One night when she was home almost an hour and a half after curfew he asked her, without yelling, "Are you having sex with Toby?"

Her parents' moralistic stance had little effect on Amanda beyond leaving her feeling more alienated from them. Their angry, judgmental position was of little use to her as she went through these important formative years. She was learning to think for herself and doing a pretty good job of it, but her mom and dad weren't focused on this, so they weren't recognizing and validating these significant developments.

At her summer camp, she and Toby were part of a splinter group of counselors and counselors-in-training who started to question some of the camp policies. Although some of their earlier strategies were not completely appropriate (a harshly mocking skit on variety night, for example, about which her parents received a memo from the camp director), this group of 15-, 16- and 17-year-olds were concerned with certain unneces-sary inequities in the staffing and labor structure. I was impressed with Amanda's sober commentary about the situation and could see she had some good points, things worth learning how to fight for. But, of course, she kept all this from Phil and Aileen because she couldn't trust how they would react.

As for their moral judgment that what she was doing was wrong and "bad," Amanda seemed completely untouched by it. She saw things differently and that was that. In fact, much of what her parents saw as "bad," she did too. But in a good way, because Toby sounded like a decent kid who was a little bit of a bad boy. "I trust my judgment," she told me. "I'm old enough to make these calls for myself."

Inevitably, Amanda started to structure her social life around concealing what she did from her parents. At times, she failed to consider whether her plans were actually safe, locked as she was in her scheming around her mom and dad. When she predicted that they would forbid her from going to a party they knew Toby would also attend (because her boyfriend was a year older, this party would be full of 16- and 17-year-olds and there would be alcohol), she kept it a secret. Instead, she asked an overly pliable neighborhood girl to invite her for a sleepover. Swearing the friend to secrecy, she snuck out close to midnight, and crossed the city by herself to attend a party with alcohol and older teens that her parents had never even heard about. With no one expecting her home.

Now things were getting unsafe.

Scary Digital Age

Rock 'n' roll may no longer panic parents, but there's now something even scarier: digital technology. Video and computer games, online activities and handheld devices can seem strange and enormously frightening to parents. Like rock 'n' roll, these new technologies are deeply attractive to kids. Like rock 'n' roll, video games shock parents' sensibilities because of how casual the sex, violence and lawlessness seem. Like rock 'n' roll, these games feel inherently threatening because they seem to come with the risk of indolence and hedonism and to pose a powerful distraction. And like rock 'n' roll, it's easy for parents to see these technologies as the enemy and to want to adopt a strongly prohibitive and controlling position.

Recently, I walked into our TV room and saw Sam sitting on the couch, laughing and talking into a headset while playing an interactive online game called *Call of Duty*. He was chasing people around and when he gunned them down with a huge machine gun, they collapsed with a splattering of blood. In some games, including the popular *Grand Theft Auto* series, kids play gangsters whose enemies are policemen whom they kill and blow up in various ways. How does a parent sit on the park bench and enjoy the show when this is the show? "Oh look, honey, our boy is barbecuing policemen with a flame thrower! Isn't that cute?"

Is there a serious level of desensitization to violence here? Maybe, although if you compare this exposure to what most children have witnessed over the long bloody course of human history, perhaps it is still not significantly more.

That said, exposure to sexually provocative imagery today is unprecedented. I mean, what kids have access to today online is really sexy, both literally and figuratively. It's served up quick and flashy. And not only is pornography more than easily available, many music videos and other forms of popular culture are grotesquely sexual.

But these changes are happening alongside others that reflect some of the great strengths of our children's generation. The tolerance for sexual differences is striking, much greater than it has ever been. In fact, in Toronto high schools, the gay–straight alliance clubs, which embrace the value of freedom of personal expression, are often the epicenter of the student body. Although we still clearly have a long way to go, our kids are perhaps the least likely generation of humans in history to judge and discriminate against difference.

Nevertheless, for many parents, seeing what our children watch on TV is deeply painful. And not just the sex and violence. When my daughter tunes in to shows that fall under the "reality TV" category—people renovating their homes, competing in beauty contests, fighting and arguing and making up with each other (it's all so fake and over the top)—I wonder: what is "real" about this? Once again, it's only natural that you begin to worry that your child's relationship to reality will be out of whack.

As concerned as parents become about the content of these TV shows, video games and other online pursuits, the form is the real concern. It's not just that they invite kids to sit on the couch and stare at a screen—and, yes, this is bad enough and childhood obesity rates are steadily growing in North America—but the quality of entertainment is so "high." You can get such a good buzz from sitting there and playing really cool games with awesome, life-like graphics that it makes the task of organizing your own fun and games out there in the real world pale by comparison. So children are losing the ability to create their own fun. More and more their expectation of receiving a high level of programming and entertainment makes the everyday opportunities for having fun—just going out and figuring out what to do by themselves—less and less attractive.

"Here we are now/Entertain us," sang Kurt Cobain in his famous anthem about this spreading teenage miasma. Written before the full advent of the digital age, in the early 1990s, "Smells Like Teen Spirit" captures not only the profound sense of entitlement to be entertained, but also what goes along with it: a turning away from the striving and competition required for success in the real world out there. In fact, even after two decades, this song remains a perfect anthem for the entitled, disengaged teenager who has withdrawn to the family rec room, retreating from the world "out there" to the world of close friends with little or no ambition. There is a word to describe this rejection of meaning and caring about things: nihilism. Reaching this point of disconnection from the world is, indeed, a catastrophic failure. Cobain, who was born the same year I was, wrote these lyrics in 1991, and killed himself three years later.

The Handheld Danger

If this isn't scary enough, we haven't even talked about what I consider the biggest danger of modern communication technology. You probably have a BlackBerry. Or an iPhone. Or an Android. These smartphones allow you to send and receive phone calls, text messages and e-mails; surf the Web; play games; download music and videos; keep personal notes, address books and schedules; and even find out where you are through GPS technology. Our children are growing up with these things. Beginning around the age of 12 or 13, many kids get a cell phone, and if they're lucky it will be one of these amazing devices, to carry with them all day long, every day. Their own personal, magical gizmo.

Smartphones will change—already have changed—the way people manage themselves emotionally. Always there, these phones provide a virtual other that a person never has to be without. Watch young people with them and you'll be amazed at how little time many of them spend without turning to that virtual other. As soon as a conversation lapses, they turn to their screens. I can feel the powerful pull to do this myself, despite not growing up with a BlackBerry. At the end of my workday, I check my e-mail, shut off the computer and leave my office. Ten steps later, I am at the elevator, where I press the button and . . . wait. No, we can't have that. I feel my hand going for my BlackBerry. What am I gonna do? Check my e-mail? I just checked it. Truth is, it's just so much easier— or is it attractive?—from a psychological perspective to check in with that little bit of wonder. My friends tell me they have the same impulse.

We are losing our ability to be by ourselves, a free-floating consciousness, free to observe and make sense of the world on our own, able to deal with the world. Psychologists call this capacity "self-regulation," the ability to manage emotionally on our own. Perhaps our children's generation (and presumably the generations that follow) will be compromised in their ability to self-regulate, and will learn to rely on having the constant presence of something to fix their attention on and to organize themselves emotionally with.

Pretty disturbing stuff. So what to do? We have to accept that some changes are bigger than us and are here to stay. Technological advancements are now so rapid that the resulting cultural changes—the ascendency of technology, the instantaneous access to knowledge, the pervasive availability of stimulation—are out of our control. It's happening whether we like it or not. This is the kind of development that takes place behind our backs; nobody is guiding it and it has its own unstoppable momentum. Our kids' generation and the generations that follow will face the challenge of figuring out what to do with a world full of individuals who are relatively unable to self-regulate.

But we are not truly helpless. To the extent that you're going to try to limit your children's use of these technologies, earlier is better. Obviously, it would be unfair (and always unsuccessful) to expose your kids to the wonders of great video game controllers and computer games in the first five years of school and then try to limit their use over the next five years. But I've met more than a few parents who are now struggling to limit their teenager's overuse of video games, and can only shake their heads and wonder what they were thinking when they excitedly bought their kids an Xbox at age 7 or 8.

Probably the best antidote is to find ways, early in our children's lives, to spend time together doing creative things in the real world that are fun, challenging and interesting. And then hope these will stand as reminders of what the virtual world can never actually deliver.

Once again, though, we must beware of the gatekeeper role. When people in the 1950s and '60s thought rock 'n' roll was "the devil's music" and tried to banish it, the main thing this did was alienate children from their parents. It certainly didn't kill Rock 'n' Roll (which I always, personally, capitalize). Hey Hey, My My, the Internet will never die.

Of course, addiction is a real concern with video games (yes, kids can and do get addicted). But back to the old catastrophic principle—until or unless it's a health issue, don't act. And if you must act, go all out: put your kid in an addiction program and remove the "drug" (Internet, computers) from the house. If your kid was becoming an alcoholic and you had booze in the house (which he started swiping) then you would get rid of it (for starters). Similarly, you need to cut off Internet access.

But short of looming catastrophic failure, you want to treat the digital menace as you do all the strange, frightening and frankly wonderful things your child will meet out there in the world. Protect his or her exposure to it in the early years and try to resist your little one's desperate pleas for better video games and cell phones, but realize as well that, with most kids, resistance is futile. Eventually they will need to participate in their world and, at a certain point, restricting their access to digital technologies and Internet content is likely depriving them of important social tools. You're right to question whether you really want to give your 10-year-old a cell phone (though at that age she's likely to tell you of a few peers who have one), but if you're not allowing her to have one by the time she's 15, you're likely making a mistake.

The Book on Facebook

Parents often ask me about Facebook, the popular social media site. Kids are supposed to be 13 before they open an account, but many do so earlier. So I hear questions about when to let a child join Facebook as well as questions about how to deal with it once the kids are users. Recently, speaking with a parents' group, one mother asked, "Would you not set rules about Facebook with a 15- or 16-year-old?"

I think I disappointed her when I said no. But there's nothing deadly or harmful about Facebook if kids use it properly. Certainly parents need to pay attention and be mindful of bullying. And as kids get older, they need to realize that those photos of teenage debauchery can hurt their chances of getting into good schools and landing coveted jobs. (This concern carries on into adulthood. One friend of mine in the financial sector decided against hiring a strong candidate whose profile photo showed him lying in a hammock with a beer in his hand. That's a bit extreme, of course—who wouldn't enjoy a little time in a hammock with a cold beer on a sunny day—but lots of young people have allowed themselves to be tagged in photos showing them in situations that would make an employer justifiably wonder about their judgment.)

"I just feel like it's such a waste of a life sitting at it," the mother responded when I repeated my mantra about not stepping in unless something catastrophic seemed to be in the offing. "I spent endless hours playing *Dungeons and Dragons* and read *Lord of the Rings* 18 times," I admitted. "I can quote large sections of those books—that's a waste of time. When we're teenagers, we fritter away the time like crazy."

Still not satisfied, she pressed on: "You wouldn't make a rule about that? We have rules about towels on the floor and putting dishes away. How is Facebook different?" I explained my distinction between a kid's life outside the house and your shared life inside the house. I consider Facebook part of life outside the house; in fact, it's now an important part of socializing and interacting with peers outside in the world. I'm not sure all parents really understand this. One mother said she didn't want her daughter getting on Facebook, preferring she have real relationships. But it is not a replacement for real relationships, it's how kids manage their real relationships.

My friends who teach in universities tell me that the achieving students—the dynamos who do well in their courses, are active in extracurricular activities and are popular with everybody— are likely to have several hundred, or even more than a thousand, friends on Facebook. The socially awkward loners are often social media refuseniks.

I don't mean this to sound like an ad for the service. It doesn't do much for me, to be honest. But I don't think parents should fear it. Instead, I suggest they join Facebook—ideally, before their kids do—and try to understand it. And once your kids join, pay attention from the park bench.

Being Interested

"So we're supposed to sit on the park bench and enjoy the show, but how are we supposed to do that when so much of what we look at is bad?" is the inevitable question I hear at this point. "How can I possibly enjoy my child when he's being rude and ugly around the house, and making really asinine decisions out there in the world? And now I'm supposed to sit back and clap?" I won't downplay the challenge parents face here. But let's be clear: when it comes to teenagers, your anger, disappointment and negative judgment can only make things worse. And that's guaranteed. So you need to find a way to get your feelings under control and get back to just being interested.

Much of what you're feeling is driven by anxiety about your kid's safety. But while parental anxiety is helpful because it makes us naturally protective of our children, we need to remember that when we feel this way, we're processing information relevant only to our own anxieties. As we vigilantly scan for information that either confirms or refutes our anxious expectations, we are less likely to notice other kinds of information.

Children, and especially adolescents, are still working out "who they are." And, not surprisingly, developing your own personal identity can be—in fact, usually is—quite a roller-coaster ride. The way parents support kids in this struggle for a solid sense of self is not so much through praise and cheerleading (to raise "self-esteem"), but through paying attention to what they're going through, witnessing their efforts and validating their experience. You need to expect the unexpected as a parent, and remind yourself that your child might surprise you (and himself) at any moment and you wouldn't want to miss it.

Daria was a perfect example of this. When she and her parents first arrived in Canada three years earlier, the family had settled in a busy Toronto neighborhood and had integrated quite well. Daria was close with both her parents and her younger brother, so it wasn't until midway through high school that the problems started. For a family unaccustomed to conflict,

the year Daria turned 16 came as a shock. She stopped studying and did badly on her first report card. She also fell in with
the "wrong crowd." Always a decent athlete and a bit of a tom-
boy, she took up skateboarding and then adopted some of the
fashion and culture surrounding it. She hung out in the park a
lot and soon wanted piercings: first in her ears (her parents said
yes), then in her nose (they said no). She smoked a little weed
and partied a bit, and her parents, Marta and Bruno, suspected
she was sexually active. Their biggest concern, though, was her
new interest in graffiti and shooting videos of her skateboard
buddies performing risky maneuvers.

The more questions her parents asked, the more evasive she
became. She lied to them about her homework and then her
teacher called to say Daria hadn't been going to class. Then the
girl started to stay out late. One night, the cops stopped her and
her gang for making films of skateboarding across a busy arte-
rial road. Next, the cops picked her up for spray painting in a
building stairwell.

That's when Marta and Bruno, panicky and upset, came to
me. In my office, we initially all sat in separate chairs, but halfway through the session, Daria (who is 5 feet, 9 inches tall) stood
up and squeezed in beside her mother on her chair. Though
Bruno looked at this with affection and warmth, there was a
lot of sadness in the room. Daria smiled, but looked chagrined
as she dismissed their concerns about the dangers of her behavior. "You bug me," she bristled at the nagging she faced. "You
hassle me and you ask me too many questions."

I told the parents to back off and give Daria some space, but
this was particularly hard for Marta. And it is difficult, especially when schools call parents demanding they do something.
Before every test, Daria and her parents fought. The teenager
was sad that the family was no longer a happy place, but she

was also deeply irritated with her parents, who were becoming more restrictive, prescriptive and inquisitive. Her school marks decreased as the active monitoring and hectoring increased. Marta talked daily with the school to find out what classes Daria attended and what her homework was. Each night, Marta called her daughter to task using this information. One night, probably the darkest moment of all, the girl told her mother to "fuck off."

Daria started avoiding home, hanging out in the 'hood, freaking out her parents. So I gave them the drill: Mom could phone the school for updates, but she couldn't act on what she learned—unless catastrophe was brewing—other than to privately share it with her husband. They also empowered the school and Daria's teachers. This plan reduced conflict in the home, but Daria's marks fell more and Marta and Bruno grew more anxious. But I explained that this is what has to happen, that it has to get worse before it gets better. When I asked them if Daria had noticed that they weren't interfering with her life anymore, they said she had. Marta recalled how her daughter had recently lingered in the kitchen after a meal, "as if she wanted something." (It was rare to see her out of her room these days.) She had complained about a Civics test the next day, and Marta had the feeling Daria wanted her to "bail her out" somehow. But she didn't come right out and say what she had on her mind and Marta, unusual for her, didn't press. This was good. "As much as she wanted you off her back," I told them, "now that you are, she wants you back."

I left my office praying there wouldn't be another incident before our next session. But when I saw them in my waiting room the next week, I could see from their faces that my prayers had not been answered. Security had nabbed Daria spray painting the stairwell of their apartment building again and had called the police.

Still, her parents stuck with my advice. Amazingly. But they realized it was definitely time for some minding. With all this not-doing, Marta and Bruno had to find a different way to be there for their daughter. They knew they had a safe "playground" in the school and those were the "climbing structures" they wanted her to work away at, but her effort there was weak. She'd even decided not to play on any sports teams that year. So they had to look outside of school to see what she was playing at. The girl was so used to her parents being intrusively interested, or parentally interested, that she was reflexively evasive. They had to be patient and earn her trust. And, to get back to our problem: the parents had to find a way to enjoy the show when there seemed so little to enjoy.

Daria had been asking her parents—"bothering" them—for a new computer and video equipment. This was not a wealthy family, so to learn that the computer they had worked so hard to buy just a few years earlier was suddenly inadequate was irritating to say the least. Her complaint that her brother was always on it and the apparent assumption that she should have her own, more powerful computer seemed more than a little entitled. But this was clearly something she cared about.

When the guidance counselor called to say Daria wanted to drop an academic class in favor of a computer course in the applied stream, the news was hard to accept, especially since Marta and Bruno wanted their daughter to go to university. But I pointed out that she was taking an interest in her academic life and they should want to support that.

Paying closer attention, Marta learned that the family computer wasn't capable of running a powerful editing program. Daria showed her an example of her work, made with this software on a friend's computer. While some of the skateboarders' stunts and wipeouts made Marta gasp, she was struck by the professionalism of the editing and music in the video. They agreed to work toward buying a new computer by the end of the year, if Daria would pay half the cost. Things warmed up a tiny bit.

Meanwhile, Bruno found cans of spray paint. Rather than confront Daria as he would have in the past, he simply asked her to move them to the basement where they should properly be stored. Bruno even built a shelf for his daughter. As he was working on it, they fell into a conversation about graffiti. Looking at all the colors, he found himself wondering about what his daughter actually did with these strange, obviously well-used pieces of equipment. Daria told him she "never tagged." Bruno had never heard the word before and asked her what she meant, and asked with real curiosity.

His question was a good one. It didn't reek of parental agenda because it flowed naturally from a father's genuine interest in his child's experiences. He was minding instead of managing and it opened up a conversation. Tagging, she explained, meant spraying your personal sign, the kind he could see on mailboxes, billboards and even trucks. Daria considered this behavior idiotic. It wasn't the vandalism that she objected to, it was the vacuous egoism of it: no talent, just spraying your "name" everywhere. "They're no better than dogs peeing on trees to mark their territory," she sneered. This made Bruno laugh. A few days later, she took him on a tour of her "work."

He was now comfortably on the bench and building trust with his daughter. And on the tour, instead of tags, he saw intricate, multicolored, abstract forms. Bruno was blown away. And Daria knew it. (This was a real "Look at you!" moment.) That summer she started a business making t-shirts with her "graffiti" designs on them. She sold them on the street and it proved a lucrative business. A year later, she enrolled at a prestigious art college.

DON'T be a gatekeeper

Avoid accepting a position that means you must either give or withhold permission for your teenager's participation in the broader world. By answering questions such as, "Dad, can I go to the party?" or "Mom, can I try out for the school volleyball team?" with a simple "yes" or "no," you're implicitly telling your child she doesn't have to think about the wisdom of her own choices, she just needs to get your permission. This interferes with the development of her understanding of and respect for reality. In addition, when you say no for good reasons, your child will focus her anger at you, not on the reasons she should be thinking about.

With teenagers, a better approach is to frame the discussion differently so she knows it's her decision. Respond as though she is informing you rather than seeking your permission. To do that, be curious and ask about the event or activity in a non-parental way (is she expecting it to be fun, what does she hope to get out of it and so on). Clearly, you will want to know when she plans to be home, but try to make it a collaborative process. Show interest and indicate that if she thinks it's a good idea, she has your support.

Of course, parents can't avoid the gatekeeping position altogether, and in the early years, the job can seem to be nothing but that ("No, you can't have that," "No, not until you put away your toys"). As your kid grows up, though, be mindful of how gatekeeping plays into her belief that worrying about reality is the parents' job ("I get to do whatever my parents say I can"). Certainly by the teen years you want your child to be responsible for her own choices in the world, with you there for support when needed. So, from the get-go, work to put her in control when it comes to dealing with the world out there. This way you can ride alongside, enjoy the show and be ready to step in and help as soon as you are needed.

DO try to hold back on digital toys and entertainment as long as possible

As offensive as you may find the content of your children's digital diversions, it's the form of these activities that should really concern us. Passive recipients of instant entertainment, always only a text away from instant contact with friends, our children run the risk of losing the ability, not to mention the inclination, to create their own fun, interpret the world through their own imaginations, and even to maintain their moment-to-moment equilibrium. For these reasons, you want to try to delay their journey into the quickly expanding alternative virtual universe.

Having said that, for most kids over 12 or 13 these days, texting, using social media such as Facebook, and sharing files and playing games over the Internet are central parts of their social worlds and you wouldn't want to deprive them of that. The solution is to play a long, slow delaying game, accepting that it's a losing battle in the long run, but fending off each step of the inevitable. If you want to reduce the chances of your children getting addicted to computer games later in childhood, you'll want to think twice about buying them the latest and greatest gaming system at age 6. They may not like it when you say no to their requests, but denying your child a game system, a cell phone, or whatever it is they hanker for, is preferable to giving it to them and then policing it.

DON'T give advice (all the time)

Well, perhaps it would be better to say "limit your advice." Children can only take so much anyway, especially in adolescence. I know I couldn't bear to have my father tell me how to do anything in my teens. Still can't, really. I'm reminded of that when I try to give advice to my own teenage son. If he doesn't outright reject it, then he looks like I am asking him to eat something highly unpleasant. Once when I desperately wanted to tell him something, he actually asked me to tell his sister instead so he could hear it without it bugging him so much. True story.

Most parental sermons are entirely unnecessary and rarely provide any new information. Dads frustrated with their teenage sons' attitude at school will tell me about the talk they had. "I told him it doesn't matter so much about the marks—although they're important in the end—it's putting in a good effort." Wow, newsflash. Or: "I explained that he has to make sure he takes the steps now that will enable him to do what he wants in the future. If he wants a lifestyle like we have in this family, it's not just going to grow on trees." No kidding. No matter how reasonable your message may be, these "conversations" are still very much parent-led moments, and as such can only end in two ways—either acquiescence and appeasement, which means he's not taking it on for himself, or defiance, which means he's not taking it on at all.

Besides, without new information, there's really nothing to be gained from such sermons, aside from possibly lowering our own anxiety. And lots of bad can come from them because they can interfere with your child's developing relationship with the problem. When you really want to offer good advice to your children, and they are clearly resistant, talk with the external authorities in their lives. They're in the perfect place to deliver information that will actually get through.

Six

Cheering Failure

When I was 6, my family went on a road trip to Prince Edward Island. We drove there, and when we got there, we drove around some more. The four of us—my three older sisters and I—were crammed into the back of the family's white Peugeot station wagon. One day we stopped at a tourist shop and I immediately fell deeply in love with a small glass vial showing the different shades of P.E.I. sand: yellow, red and orange. "Can I have it?" I asked my mom. She said no.

I always started with my mom and then, if I needed to, I went to my dad. But he also said no. I was practiced at the art of splitting even then, though I wasn't always successful: I pleaded with both of them, but they remained unmoved by my desire.

So I just took it.

We climbed back in the car and rattled along for a while, but that beautiful treasure sitting in my shorts pocket kept calling to me. Finally, my impulse to admire it overcame my fear of being caught and I surreptitiously (I thought) pulled it out to take a peek. You try doing this while you're squished in the back seat with three sisters. Of course, they immediately busted me. "Dad! He stole that thing!"

A moment later we were driving back to the scene of the crime. My dad led me inside and I will never forget his words as he explained why we were there again: "Look what he had in his hot little hand." It wasn't just the word "hot" that made that line burn so deeply, it was my father's disappointment in me. I can feel the shame even now.

But as humiliated as I was in front of my father (and seriously angry at him because of it), the woman who ran the store really intimidated me. She asked me if I understood what I had done and if I realized how serious an offense I'd committed. Her serious tone and the words she chose—criminal, police, jail—scared the bejeebers out of me.

If I'd been in the first world of guilt and shame with my father, this external authority sent me quickly into the second world, the terribly frightening world of reality. I left the store fully convinced that what I'd done was truly stupid.

I knew I had failed in my father's eyes, and this knowledge left me feeling guilty and ashamed. No doubt my face still burned when I got back in the car, and I certainly didn't look at or speak to my sisters. Yet the shopkeeper's words had a different effect altogether. She'd made me feel anxious, so I left the store thinking something like, "Phew! Close one." With a sense of relief, in other words. But I'd learned something and I'd learned it through a particular kind of failure: a painful moment at the hands of an external authority.

To survive in our world—which now rarely involves literal survival—children need to learn a great deal. It's a good thing they have about 20 years to get the job done because it does take a lot of training to prepare to thrive in our complex, fast-paced and distraction-filled world. The failures they need are the kinds that occur in the social institutions they operate in as children, which is where they get to practice being a member of society: schools, camps, sports teams, community centers—or, as in my case, souvenir stores. The way they relate to the rules and expectations of those institutions and, more important, to the adults who enforce them, is a blueprint for how they will enter the adult world. For teenagers, in particular, the essential equivalent of the scraped knee is failure at the hands of an external authority. So failing a test after not studying, not being allowed to go on a field trip because of past misbehavior, not being asked back to camp as a counselor because of a lack of maturity, or being dressed down by a scary store clerk are the kinds of failures that orient children to reality, get their attention and make it more likely that they will attend to these things more carefully in the future.

Teenage Wasteland

Jake was a master at playing his divorced parents against each other. Terri and Paul had split when their son was 3 and Jake, an only child, had long used that to his advantage. Recently, after a fight with his mom, who'd been trying to set some limits on his behavior, the 16-year-old announced: "Fine! Then I'm living with Dad." And so he moved into his father's condo.

When Jake was a boy, he'd been able to talk his dad into buying and doing just about anything he wanted. "Time with Dad is fun time," Terri would later tell me, as she lamented that she had to play bad cop to Paul's good cop. But when it came to actually living with Dad, the teenager found his old man not that easy to manipulate. And so, after only a month, he moved back to his mom's house.

But his time away hadn't helped his demeanor and soon his treatment of Terri deteriorated to the point that the neighbors started to worry about her safety. She lived in a semi-detached and one night Jake's yelling and abusive language was so bad that one of the men who lived next door came over and pushed his way past Terri as she opened the door. "That's enough!" he said, confronting the boy. "Don't ever talk to your mother like that again, or I am calling the cops."

That's when Terri came to see me. Jake, it turned out, had a long history of difficult and defiant behavior. Two years earlier, she'd taken him to another psychologist for an assessment over concerns about a possible learning disorder, which might have helped explain his powerful reluctance to engage in school. But he refused to participate in the assessment. (This is actually relatively rare, especially with this psychologist, a man I respected and knew was experienced with reluctant teenagers.) My colleague's conclusion: "Dad needs to step in to protect Mom."

Jake smoked a lot of pot and had an immature and simplistic identification with marijuana culture and the adolescent trappings of "cool." Bob Marley emanated from his iPod all day long. He liked to project a cool image, but Jake was in fact emotionally quite fragile. Most of the time, he maintained an imperious attitude toward his social life—they were his friends, his "boys," and he could do what he wanted with them. But occasionally his boys weren't so much his at all, and Jake would return home furious at some slight or exclusion. Terri had the impression that he worked hard at maintaining his status in the group and feared he might, in fact, be a bit of a fringe member. When things went south in Jake's social life, he went back home to his mom and regressed. Sometimes this meant he dissolved in tears—perhaps lamenting how horrible his life was, or how useless he was. These were deeply disturbing moments for Terri, who found ways to soothe and reassure him. Or he became physically clingy, as if he were retreating back to a baby state. Then, the next day, Jake could well be back to his disrespectful, demanding self. It was as if the childish display of the night before had never happened, and the idea of cool Jake with the cool friends had returned.

To both Terri and Paul, therefore, he appeared terribly fragile. They were aware how precarious his self-image was, and how much of what sustained him was a fantasy of who he was. When this fantasy clashed with reality and it all fell apart, Jake would come home raging at the world—and his parents had no idea how to respond. These were true Story of Woe moments: yes, he was hurting because the disappointment with his friends was all too real, but there was also something in his approach that suggested he was trying to avoid the realities of what had actually happened, preferring to return to a familiar and safe place with his mother. When he came home complaining about a "mean" teacher, Terri (and Paul, too, during those times that Jake stayed at his dad's) struggled between a wish to be understanding and not wanting to be conned by Jake's notion that the problem was the teacher.

Sixteen years old, and a student at a public high school, Jake was struggling with many of his courses. He skipped classes often, had terrible sleeping habits, rarely if ever studied or did homework, and regularly failed to complete or hand in assignments. Although he had been a reluctant, disengaged student for many years, he was in danger of failing his year. But his parents were also deeply concerned about his behavior in their homes.

At my invitation, Terri and Paul came in together. It was one of the few times they'd been in the same room since their separation, and they willingly acknowledged that they'd not worked well together over the years and that their communication had been poor. They also agreed that Jake had a dismaying level of entitlement. He seemed to feel he should just get anything he wanted: money, take-out food, skateboards, whatever. Especially skateboard shoes, apparently; after I asked them to do an inventory between the two houses, they discovered 11 pairs. And yet he did next to no housework, and when he did, his procrastination drove his mom and dad nuts.

Because Jake was an unusually skinny kid, Terri couldn't stop worrying about his eating habits. She bought him the foods he asked for and, when he left those uneaten, bought the next ones he asked for in hopes that he might eat something. He refused to go grocery shopping with either of them and then raged at them when the foods he wanted weren't available. He often didn't even show up for dinner or would leave just before Terri served it—sometimes, he went hungry and sometimes, she discovered, he opted to go to his dad's, where he could just order a pizza.

United We Stand; Divided We Fall

As Terri and Paul admitted that their lack of coordination and communication contributed to the problems, they started to realize an inescapable rule in parenting: united we stand, divided we fall. When parents are not coordinated in their responses, children can exploit the cleavage in ways that are ultimately not good for them. Kids will often look for "splitting" opportunities, precisely because they are weak spots where they can gain influence and control.

Like Jake, 11-year-old Gemma was an expert at splitting her parents. She'd had trouble adjusting to school since the first grade. She was obviously bright; her parents, Annie and Martin, had even had her tested to see if she was gifted (she wasn't, but she was above average). Gemma started off enthusiastic about school and was excited about the other students. But after some initial success, including making some "best friends," things soured. Within a month, she was complaining about the teacher and the other kids, who she said were mean and didn't treat her fairly. The same sequence of events took place in the second grade and it became so bad that Gemma started refusing to go to school. When she told her parents she was being "bullied," they moved her to a new school where she stayed for two years—until she was so unhappy with her classmates that Annie and Martin moved her again.

In the sixth grade, during her second year at her third school, Gemma was once again struggling with her peers and saying she hated school. One night she told her parents she hated her life because she was always being bullied. Annie and Martin reacted differently to this story. Annie was distressed to hear that the bullying had started again, and wondered out loud what the school was doing about it. Martin, who'd suspected that the first bullying incident four years earlier was as much Gemma's doing as anything else, was less sympathetic. Gemma seemed to sense this because it was a familiar split between her parents. As they talked about it in the living room, the girl snuggled into her mother's side, shielding her eyes from her father and slowly becoming mute.

Later, the couple fell into a familiar argument. Martin accused his wife of being "sucked in" by Gemma's dramatics, and Annie became upset with her husband's "lack of compassion" for the girl's suffering. "You need to show her that you care about her," she pleaded. But this just seemed to make Martin angrier: the implication that his deep concern about Gemma's inability to deal with problems represented a lack of caring felt highly unfair. And inaccurate. If anything, Annie's responses to both Gemma and him made him even less inclined to be sympathetic. He became even more unsympathetic to balance out what he viewed as Annie's over-responsiveness. The reverse was true as well: Annie, observing Gemma's unhappy, cowering response to her dad's disapproval, became more inclined to comfort and sympathize with her. A vicious cycle developed with Annie's empathy deepening Martin's suspicion, and his lack of compassion deepening her solicitousness. The softer Annie became, the harder Martin became. And vice versa.

They were both right, of course. As with all Stories of Woe, Gemma was genuinely suffering emotionally so she needed some parental compassion, but she was also avoiding reality and spinning stories designed to recruit her parents to her cause. It isn't either/or—either she's sucking her parents in, or she's really suffering—it's both. And Gemma needed both her parents to see this, so that they could both respond to both sides of the communication, rather than get split on them.

The picture, however, was even more complicated because Gemma had a little brother, 7-year-old Rufus, with whom she rarely got along. Rufus was witness to many of his sister's struggles, and when there was an issue with Gemma, he often took a background role, slipping quietly off to the TV room or even his bedroom to play on his own. His dad often joined him there, not infrequently irritated at both his daughter and his wife. As we talked about this together, Martin and Annie agreed that some subtle alliances had developed in the family: Martin and Rufus, Annie and Gemma. When the family was operating under these alliances, they realized, other important relationships—Martin and Annie's marital relationship, for example, and Gemma and Rufus's sibling relationship—became strained, or "didn't work" in Martin's frank terms.

That's why, for these two, fixing things in their family included focusing on their own relationship. Although still a solid team when it came to the details of their busy and demanding family lives, they both acknowledged that under the strain of the parenting job, together with the alienating effect of being split over Gemma, their relationship was not at its best. Reinvesting energy in their marriage and feeling closer to each other was an essential part of their ability to resist their pattern of splitting.

Annie recognized that by splitting them, Gemma had found a way to avoid accepting the reality of her situation. The reality was that she could not always be the queen bee, disappointment at school is part of the deal, and not everyone is going to be your best friend all the time. These are lessons every kid should have learned long before the sixth grade, but Gemma hadn't, partly because she'd been able to avoid this education by retreating to her family and crying woe. Martin recognized that when he responded in a negative and critical manner, he was intimidating to Gemma and not helpful to her.

Interestingly, it wasn't Gemma who protested the introduction of a "date night"—it was Rufus. He let it be known that he was deeply unhappy with the idea of his parents going out once a week while the children stayed home, subjected to the evil horrors of a babysitter. His final attempt to communicate this to his parents on the first week was a full-out temper tantrum as they extricated themselves and wished the poor babysitter good luck. The extent of Rufus's regressive display was a striking change in the family, since it was usually Gemma who freaked out about things. Seeing her brother in this role for a change may have been a relief for her; after all, he was the younger of the two. Or maybe seeing how embarrassing these displays actually were gave her something to think about when it came to her own conduct at home. Whatever it was, as the parents became more united, Gemma's emotional outbursts slowly diminished. She also got along with her brother a bit better, since they were now forced to share the TV once a week without their parents around. Somehow they worked it out.

The Two-Headed Parenting Monster

Stories such as Jake's and Gemma's are why I often have to help parents return to the traditional family structure of Mom and Dad at the top, in control and in sync, and the kids—the citizens—waiting to learn what the policies are. Successfully withstanding efforts at splitting is essential for this to work. When it does, the parents may be a bit exasperating to the kids (because the kids now have to toe the party line), but they are firmly in control in a way that is emotionally containing to children.

In Gemma's family, Martin and Annie's reconnecting was critical to turning things around, but in families where parents are separated or divorced, such as Jake's, this isn't possible. So the first thing Paul and Terri addressed was coordinating their efforts better. To help them, I had them make a basic distinction between Jake's life outside their two homes and his life inside their homes. Outside included school and socializing (and, yes, even sex and drugs and video games). Inside pertained to their shared life together: chores, respectful treatment of housemates, meeting responsibilities. Outside, they were to sit on the park bench; inside, they had to be authoritative and in control.

To accomplish this, they did the following:

1. Made a clear, but finite, list of expectations that applied to both houses.

    Clear meant the tasks had to be fully defined (for example, doing the dishes includes wiping the counter). Finite meant it had to be short and they couldn't keep adding to it. Here's the list they came up with:

- Take the garbage (including the recycling) to the curb every week.

- Put his own dishes in the dishwasher (scrape and rinse first).

- Put his dirty laundry in the basement and pick it up when it's clean.

- Replace toilet paper when necessary.

This list might seem puny, especially since most of us probably had a much longer list of expectations when we were growing up. But I always caution parents to keep their first attempts at this modest so they set themselves up for success. Immediately jumping to a level of domestic responsibility we remember from our own childhoods will lead most parents directly to failure. Keeping the list short and clear increases your chances of actually getting it to stick.

2. Calculated how much money they were giving him each week.

They'd been operating on a simple "parent as ATM" basis and, between them, they discovered they were giving him about a hundred bucks a week. If, like me, you're wondering what he'd been spending it on, here goes: $10 a day for lunch, "skateboard money," hoodies, Bob Marley t-shirts and, of course, pot. The fact that Jake was starved for cash was a useful point of leverage for his parents (it isn't always, because some kids just don't seem to care about money as much as others).

3. Agreed on a once-a-week allowance of $80 (half from Paul, half from Terri).

   He earned this only by meeting the list of inside-the-house expectations—and though they didn't put it this way, he could skip his classes and still get his allowance as long as he was a "good citizen" at home.

Basically, they offered Jake a deal: "We're going to treat you with more respect when it comes to your life out there in the world. We trust that you will figure it out, so we will give you space, be careful about making negative judgments and generally stay out of your face. In exchange, we're asking for more respect around our homes." This is an arrangement most teenagers are pretty happy to accept, whatever language the parents find to communicate it. Terri also phoned Jake's school and gave the staff the three-part message: entrust, inform and empower. If nothing else, this helped lower her anxiety.

One evening, Jake fought with his mom after ignoring her request that he either be home by midnight or at least report in by then. He left for his dad's place late at night. Jake did not have his own key—he just expected his dad to open up as he always did. But his dad was out of town. Discovering he was locked out, Jake texted his mom: along with a lot of swearing about his father, he demanded that she pick him up.

In the past, she would have picked him up. But now that she and Paul were "working on the same team," as she put it, stepping back was easier. "Before, I might have been partly angry at Paul, or else maybe worried that he'd accuse me of leaving Jake in an unsafe position," she said. So she didn't even answer Jake's text. Feeling more certain of Paul's support and their parental solidarity helped Terri resist the powerful pull to respond. When Jake showed up at her house—again without a key—and pounded on the door, she sleepily opened it up for him and went back to bed, ignoring his complaints.

Next, Jake lost his bus pass, and the tasks required to replace it made him "really tense." Although she was tempted to take care of it for him, Terri just reviewed what he needed to do to get a new one. But as it became clear to Jake that his mom was not going to step in as she'd always done in the past (this was, after all, outside-the-house stuff), his anxiety spiked. When he started shouting and swearing at her, she was terrified because it reminded her of the bad old days, not so very long ago. Still, she didn't swerve from her course; instead, she left the house.

Meanwhile, they had some initial challenges with the new allowance system. At one point, when Terri asked Jake to put his dishes away, he tried to turn the tables on her: "I'm not gonna do little chores unless you give me money." Fortunately, she remembered my advice about not engaging him in such arguments: "Less is more," she said to herself. The dishes sat there all evening, but before she went to bed, Terri noticed that Jake had quietly loaded them in the dishwasher. As teenagers begin to yield to the inevitable, parents must pay as little attention to their yielding as possible, which helps them save face. Terri wisely said nothing, and when the time came, she gave Jake his allowance.

As Paul and Terri stepped out of their old over-available modes and forced Jake to feel the consequences of his actions, he experienced a series of small but painful "failures." Neglecting to inform his mom of when he might be home for dinner now meant that he had to make something from the fridge—out of the disgusting adult food she kept in there. Deciding to say "screw this" and taking off to Dad's without first thinking about his own finances (he was broke, carrying only his newly restored bus pass) now meant getting to Dad's, being refused any money until allowance day, and having to make something from a fridge with an even smaller selection of disgusting adult food.

Within two months, Terri and Paul began to see the first signs of improvement. Although Jake's attitude toward school remained unchanged, things were considerably better at home. For one thing, they no longer supervised his homework so there was less to fight about. But their success at uniting their parenting efforts, and Jake's repeated unpleasant experiences, worked their magic. He became a more reasonable citizen, more likely to check in about meals, and text ahead of time when he was changing plans. As these efforts led to more successful outcomes, he started to become more pleasant and even respectful in his conduct. He was home for dinner more often and was more likely to eat what Terri or Paul served. He was also more affectionate, suddenly giving his mom kisses on leaving and returning. These were a new kind of kiss—affectionate, but not clingy. Jake's regressive moments became less frequent. He was feeling more mature, and was beginning to like this feeling. He liked being more emotionally separate from his mother—in this way she could see him for who he was becoming: a man. He felt good knowing she saw him this way. It was as if a little of the childish entitlement had faded away to be replaced by its opposite: a little mature appreciation.

External Authority

When Jake's parents stopped feeding into his power trips, he discovered that trying to ignore all reasonable codes of conduct—even just being uncooperative and assuming things would be fine—resulted in bad outcomes. This is stuff he should have glommed onto long before the age of 16, but he was behind. And so he was learning about reality in the most basic way: if you don't think about food ahead of time, you go hungry. It didn't take long for Paul and Terri to sort this out because once they reinstated themselves as the government in the family, the citizen fell into line. But Jake still had a ways to go, the big scary world was still waiting for him and there were more painful moments ahead. There had to be. While things were operating more reasonably at home, Jake still had to figure things out vis-à-vis the authorities out there in the external world.

Unfortunately, the same cultural shift that has led to over-parenting has neutered the power of external authorities. If I needed a reminder of this, I certainly received it when my son Sam tried shoplifting 35 years after I had. My wife was furious. "You deal with him!" she fumed. Sam trailed behind her, tears streaked down his face. In his hot little hand was a container of orange Tic Tacs.

So I took him back to Honest Ed's, a famous and colorful Toronto discount store. He had a little jar he kept his allowance in and I told him he could either give his loot back or buy it—either way, he had to apologize for stealing it. As Sam approached the elderly woman at the checkout, she smiled an indulgent smile worthy of a doting grandmother. Poor Sam: as he put the stolen goods on the counter and started his apology, his shame overcame him and he burst into tears. What did the clerk do? She cried, "Oh, you poor baby. You can keep the Tic Tacs!" And then she looked at me with contempt, as if to say, "You ogre!"

While I can't claim that there weren't sweet old cashiers like this when I was a kid, there is no debate that external authority figures have lost their authority—often, as in this case, they've just given it away. The dynamics at Honest Ed's mirror those between children and teachers, coaches, camp counselors, police and even neighbors. Too often, these external authorities look to parents to provide the solution—just when we need the out-siders to step in.

Part of the problem is that entitled adults don't respect the authority of others. After the Avalanche midget junior A hockey team cut two young players at tryouts, for example, two sets of parents launched lawsuits against the team and the Greater Toronto Hockey League. According to the statement of claim from one of the fathers, the defendants "caused irreparable psychological damage" to the boy's "self-esteem as an impres-sionable teenager and demoralized [him] as an athlete and team hockey player with his peers. The conduct by all defendants destroyed the dignity of my son, whom [sic] in good conscience gave his team nothing but his best efforts."

That's an extreme example, of course, but it shows how over-parenting serves to neuter the external authorities in our society. These figures are now too intimidated to play the role we need them to play. But that story of parental entitlement also reveals a fundamental misunderstanding of what is good and bad for children. Being cut from a sports team is not harmful to kids; indeed, the experience should almost be a requirement of childhood.

Beyond Praise

Just as many parents misunderstand the value of failure, and the essential role of authority figures, they also often misunderstand praise. Alice was a young mother who suffered from postpartum depression during her son's first year. When Ryan was 4, Alice came to me looking to repair the rocky relationship that had developed between them after that difficult start. As we talked in my office, and Ryan played with a bin of toys I keep there, she frequently responded to his play with positive and enthusiastic comments: "Good work," "That's so excellent," "I'm so proud of you." But I could see how Ryan was using the toys in play sequences that involved threatening figures attacking frightened, vulnerable ones. Alice's comments weren't attuned to his play, to a degree that was almost jarring. Her comments were bright and positive, while Ryan had the T-Rex slowly devour the mommy doll head-first. Alice's comments weren't building Ryan's self-esteem, as she hoped. Instead, they frustrated him. Eventually he became so annoyed that he threw one of the toys at his mother. Then she said nothing.

Naturally, Alice wanted Ryan to develop good self-esteem, but she also, unconsciously perhaps, wanted quite desperately to be a participant in his development and feel validated as his mother. But her own desires were interfering with her ability to see what her son needed from her, and her praise frustrated him rather than making him feel proud or happy. Gradually, as Alice focused more on the meaning of his play—as she became more focused on him and less driven by her need to be a good mother—Ryan became less defiant and angry, and eventually the two were able to play together in a way that both of them enjoyed.

This is what can go wrong when the pressure to be a good mother leads a parent to overuse an otherwise sensible strategy such as praise. But what was so alarming with Alice and Ryan was how her need to please him made her overly vulnerable to his demands—and that offered him a chance to obtain a frightening level of control. Alice's need for his acceptance and approval had both scared Ryan and undermined his mother's value to him. Alice had lost, at least temporarily, her status as someone able to recognize and affirm him. In her need to be his mother, she had lost his respect. This was obviously painful for her but, worse, by winning the battle for power with his mother, he lost what he most needed.

Not all my cases are as dramatic as that one, but it's clear that many parents make the mistake of taking a particular recommended practice too far. They believe they must praise children in order to build self-esteem, but when their best intentions become a reflex and they routinely offer praise, regardless of the context, they devalue it. When children repeatedly hear that they are so special, they begin to take it for granted. That's why the well-meaning practice of giving trophies to every kid on the soccer team is so misguided. And university professors and bosses are seeing a generation raised on unlimited praise, young adults who expect constant approval and don't accept constructive criticism well.

Overused, praise is also easily caught up in the dynamics of control between adults and children. Praise is a gift in the sense that the adult intends to say, "I like you. I think you're great." This initiates an exchange in which the next move is for the child to give something back: to accept the praise, implicitly praising the parent in return. When the child grins and looks pleased, he is saying: "You're important to me and your praise feels good."

This response feels good. We feel rewarded by it. And, as every parent quickly learns, the child who is eager to please is much more manageable and likeable. So we use praise not just to develop self-esteem in our kids, but, sometimes, to secure legitimacy and control. In the old days, before adults thought about their children this way, when they held a kind of tyranny over them, they didn't worry about such things. Since today's parent must be much more creative to establish an authoritative position, this method of gaining influence is all the more tempting.

As emotionally nutritious as praise might be to developing self-esteem, it isn't what's most essential to children. There's a crucial difference between praise and recognition. While praise responds only to the wish to be seen as "good," recognition validates children as separate individuals with specific qualities and characteristics. And, as the word suggests, it is not about saying anything in particular—or even anything at all. It is about reflecting on a child and seeing what he or she is expressing. By recognizing a kid, a parent says, with or without words: "Yes, I see you. You are showing me that you are big and strong." Or love animals. Or feel angry with me. Or whatever the child is trying to communicate.

When Alice focused on recognizing the meaning in Ryan's play rather than simply praising his efforts, she began to occupy a more helpful place in his world. By merely paying close attention to his aggressive play, she communicated, "You're telling me about feeling angry and fierce. You don't want to feel vulnerable, you want to feel strong." Recognizing children in this way helps avoid the routine praise that leads children to take it for granted. Perhaps more important, it helps us understand why our children are vying for our attention beyond the need to feel they have accomplished something "good."

In spite of all I've said about the need for children to experience painful, non-catastrophic failures, we don't actually want our kids to fail in the long run. Getting out of the praise business helps here too, because it's a way of moving past the pass–fail or good–bad binary. It's remarkably easy for many parents to fall into this trap. They keep saying, "Oh, that's beautiful!" and "Aren't you clever!" when there are so many other options beyond good and bad. Just being interested is what's important. "Wow, what's that?" is a way to steer away from the pressures of being good and clever, and into the much more important realm of actually having something to say.

Chapter Six

Everyone Screws Up

"Things will get worse before they get better," I reminded Paul
and Terri as they continued to leave Jake to his own devices at
school. When you're relying on painful, non-catastrophic failure
to work its magic, this is inevitable. And like many parents, Terri
struggled with this, especially when it came to Jake's attendance
and performance at school. "He's sleeping in until 11 a.m., noon,
even 1 p.m. I'm supposed to just leave him there?" Just leaving
him there proved too much for her. Afraid he was still in bed,
she called home from work and when he finally picked up, she
urged him to get up and go to school. "You promised me you
weren't going to bug me about that," he yelled at her. Terri was
too sweet to tell me how much she must have hated me that day.

Meanwhile, Paul arranged a job in the pro shop at his golf
club for Jake. I admit I had serious misgivings about this; when
parents find employment for their kids, it becomes so easy to
carry the worry ball because they don't want to inconvenience
their connection. But Paul made a point of not supervising and
Jake didn't miss a shift, showed a good attitude on the job and
was beginning to feel pretty good about the work and the pay.
Some good fellowship was developing between the boy and his
dad over working and earning money—the world of grown-ups.
And their shared interest in golf and the time they spent together
in the masculine milieu of the club meant some important male
bonding was also taking place.

Things continued to be remarkably better at home. But when
Terri called Jake's guidance counselor, her check-in person at
the school, she was disheartened to learn that Jake was skipping
more classes than ever and had missed two important tests. She
relayed this information to Paul but otherwise didn't act on it.
Several days later Jake admitted that he'd missed the tests. In

the past, he'd only talked about school when she prompted him with a "Shouldn't you be studying for your math test?" This time he brought it up, and instead of being angry at the teachers, he expressed frustration with himself. To Terri, his reaction seemed both similar to his regressive moments in the past—he was tearful and somewhat despairing in tone—but also different. For one thing, he stopped short of calling himself useless, and he didn't seem to be completely collapsing. This time it seemed more an expression of his frustration with himself. "Why do I always put things off?" he lamented. Rhetorically, Terri supposed.

She felt compelled to step in and help him with his feelings to some extent (this was all new to him in a certain way), but I'd forewarned her that as reality begins to kick in, kids will attempt to bring down their anxiety level by "hooking" their parents in. Unfortunately, Jake had to stay anxious. When his parents had proven that they were truly back on the park bench, Jake went through a period of trying to get them off it again. He tried, for example, to flaunt his lack of caring about school and marks in an effort to ignite Terri's anxiety. "I got a 31 on my history test, but whatever," he announced, in a show of nonchalance. Terri refused to take the bait. Without even looking up from her book, she blandly replied, "That's too bad." When Paul told Jake that the school had called reporting his absence, there was a pause, and then the teenager said, "Whatever. I don't care about school anyway. It's useless." This was Paul's chance to take the bait. But he didn't. In fact, he didn't say anything at all.

This "I don't care" strategy is actually a common one, and something young children often attempt in their efforts to manage their parents. It's the cutting-off-your-nose-to-spite-your-face strategy. Children are ingenious because this approach plays on the parental fear of failure so effectively. When the 7-year-old can't have the action figure he wants, he says, "Fine. Then I'm not going to do my homework." As if doing homework is something that benefits his parents (which it does to the extent that they're carrying the worry ball). Many parents, in the heat of the moment, actually fail to see through this ruse and may even feel it necessary to up the ante. "Okay, fine," they say. "Then you're not going to the sleepover this weekend." Wrong. That's just rising to the bait and indicating that you can't let the failure occur. Terri and Paul had to prove they weren't about to pick up the worry ball again.

This "cult of casual parenting," as Terri called it, did not feel right at all. (What cult? I wondered.) Not being more active in Jake's academic life felt irresponsible. "Exams are coming up and I see it escalating," she told me. "How can I just say nothing? When you see the signs, you're supposed to do something." But she was doing "something"—she was paying attention to him, noticing what he was up to and thinking about it, ready to respond when necessary and validate what was important to him.

Sure enough, she soon noticed that Jake was meeting his parents' expectations at home, was into his job and concerned not to be late. Even her friends had started remarking on his new attitude; one described him as a "different kid." Terri saw that he was opening up to people, and not just if they were "cool."

That was on the home front, though. I was glad to hear how he'd learned from his domestic failures, but I predicted that he would soon suffer some academic ones (though I didn't tell his parents that). I wasn't surprised when Terri called with "a bit of an emergency." Jake had had a meltdown the night before an exam, but after crying and moaning about it he actually went upstairs and appeared to study for a few hours. In the morning, as he headed off to school, Terri wished him luck. Her hope took a dive a few hours later, though, because the school called: Jake had not shown up for his exam. I counseled her to say little. This was a non-catastrophic, but definitely painful, error and Jake would soon have to face his problems with avoidance.

As it turned out, she didn't need my advice. The school called the next day to say that Jake had written his exam after all. Instead of taking it in the regular room with the rest of his class, he'd chosen to sit in a private space with a proctor. This was something he was entitled to do because of his learning disability, but he'd never taken advantage of the option before because of his reluctance to acknowledge his difficulties. He had not only written his exam, he had taken on his school problems for himself.

He'd also moved on emotionally. He accepted that he had limitations and dealt with them. The reality is, we all make mistakes. Learning this had helped Jake move into the second world, where mistakes and failures were inconvenient and to be minimized, but unavoidable.

Yes, we all make mistakes, even parents—another lesson I learned that summer in P.E.I. In the end, I had my revenge. Leaving the island in our station wagon, I heard my parents discussing their strategy as we inched our way forward in the lineup for the ferry. The sign said children under 10 were free and I heard my dad suggest that he'd just claim that all four kids in the back were under 10, even though my two older sisters were not. As the car rolled up to the ticket booth and my dad rolled down his window, I was ready.

"Two adults and four kids under 10," my dad said.

"No, there's not!" I yelled. "Two kids are over 10. He's lying!"

I'd learned my lesson: out here in reality, we all have to follow the same rules.

Revenge is sweet.

DO cheer (privately) for painful, non-catastrophic failure

The "privately" here is obviously crucial, but the truth is, you don't want your child to go through his or her childhood without getting roughed up by reality. Of course, the cheering is actually often a bit impossible, but remember that if the failure is commensurate with her age and stage, it will be a good thing in the end. The time when this rather odd idea is especially true is when a child is hoping to avoid accepting some aspect of reality. For example, a 10-year-old says "I don't care" when her parents point out that if she doesn't do her homework she will fail the assignment (let's call this reality). You could fight her on this, and maybe after an evening of yelling and tears the thing would more or less get done, or you could not fight her and let reality teach her in the morning. Make sure you have a teacher who knows you trust him to fail your daughter. The last thing you want is her learning that she can get away with such a lousy effort.

DON'T always praise

It's easy to mistake recognizing children's efforts, and paying attention to them, with praising them. In the last 25 years particularly, the increased concern over children's "self-esteem" has led many parents and other childcare providers to draw the overly simple conclusion that repeatedly telling a child how good he is will foster a sense inside of him that he is good. In fact, the opposite is often the case—repeatedly using praise as a parenting strategy reduces the value of praise.

But the biggest problem with responding to kids with praise is it means that other ways of responding don't occur. Praise places a child's efforts on a good–bad continuum, meaning there is an implicit evaluative component to it that is easily tied up with parents' own agendas for their child. Beyond praise, there are ways to focus on what a child is doing or saying, as opposed to how good it is. "Wow, tell me about your picture" can lead to a far more interesting exchange with a child than "Wow, what a beautiful picture. Good for you!" which will generally stop the conversation right there.

DO require respect for rules inside your home

Make a distinction between your child's life outside the home, including school, and your shared life inside your home. Outside the home, try to remain in the supportive bystander role as much as possible: unless things are happening that make catastrophic failure a concern, avoid making rules and demands, especially in the teenage years, so that your child learns that outside the home stuff is his problem, but that Mom and Dad are always right there with a vote of confidence or a helping hand. Inside the house, though, things should be the other way around. There should be a clear and finite (not too long and not forever growing) list of responsibilities and expectations, which each member of the family is required to live up to.

Be authoritative, in-control parents where the family's shared life together is concerned. Household expectations should apply to everyone (no abusive language, for example) and you should make an effort to ensure that everyone follows the rules. If you respectfully stand back from directing your child's outside responsibilities you'll actually find that inside-the-home success is easier to achieve. Not only does it reduce the number of conflicts and battles in many cases, but it also means you are making a kind of respect exchange; in effect, you are saying: we will respect your choices out there in the world, and in exchange, we're asking for more respect around the house. This exchange tends to work because not guiding and directing a teenager's efforts, while staying tuned in and interested, sets the tone for a more mature relationship. When you see your child in more adult ways, it tends to pull for more adult behavior at home. Of course, the reverse is also true: interfering and negatively judging his efforts out in the world is patronizing and will lead to less mature, more childish functioning inside your home.

Seven

Disabilities, Disorders and Disasters

Paying attention had been a problem for Philippe since kindergarten. By age 14, when he was in his first year of high school, his problem was so severe that he was barely keeping his head above water. His school struggles weren't new, but with the increased academic demands of high school and the new task of keeping track of eight different courses with eight different teachers, his marks plummeted. His locker was a mess; his binders were completely hopeless.

His mother, Simone, was used to knowing Philippe's teachers, and knowing them well. Since the beginning she had been ensuring that her son stayed on track, and inevitably, by the end of the year, this meant that she and the teacher had become familiar with coordinating the various issues that children have to deal with over the course of their development: learning to sit still and pay attention; learning to remember things; learning to read; learning how to plan, write, and construct projects; learning how to write essays. Each of these steps, and countless others in between, proved highly challenging for the boy. Simone and her husband, Arturo, found themselves constantly stepping in, anticipating Philippe's upcoming projects and overseeing his efforts. There seemed no other option.

The homework had started coming home in the first grade in the form of a recommendation from the teacher that they read every night with Philippe, even for just a few minutes. This recommendation, by the way, is advisable in every way. It's not just good for kids' learning, it's also good for their attitude toward learning, which is even more important. It's fun, so early on children associate reading with pleasure. And when it works, it works really well. In many cases, for example, this "educational recommendation" gets incorporated into a family's bedtime ritual—snack, bathroom, bed—where we get to snuggle into the blankets and read a favorite and often extremely familiar book. And so it's a great way for parents to connect emotionally with their kids as well.

But for Simone and Arturo, this never happened. Neither of them were big readers, so before they received this excellent advice, their family's nighttime routines had been very different and their attempts to initiate a reading period had failed. From the beginning, "helping" Philippe with these issues had meant battling him over these issues. And by high school this had taken a toll on all three of them, and his relationship with his mother, in particular, had deteriorated considerably.

Growing up, Philippe had been a happy, energetic kid, but also restless and fidgety. He'd always enjoyed his friends and often thought of hilarious things to say or do to them. But all his teachers had had trouble reining him in. Early in his school career, his parents noticed that he had a hard time remembering things and organizing himself, in even the most basic ways. Simone and Arturo were forever scrambling to hand in forms they'd just found out about so Philippe could go on the soccer trip, for which he'd forget his shoes, but which Mom could, of course, drop off. In the primary grades he found himself in the principal's office much more often than most kids. By the end of elementary school, he'd developed a bit of a—well, hate would be too strong a word—but certainly a dislike for school, "work" and most teachers.

An assessment in the third grade suggested that Philippe met the criteria for a diagnosis of ADHD, though the assessor was reluctant to say so definitively, suggesting that there were also signs of "attitudinal" problems, reflected in Philippe's fights with his parents and teachers. The psychologist suggested he might have what's known as Oppositional Defiant Disorder (ODD).

At this time, the family's battles revolved almost entirely around trying to get Philippe to do his assignments. He was at a competitive private school and there was homework to be done every day. Simone had instituted a study period for both Philippe and his younger sister, Julie. Initially, her rule was that no one was allowed on a screen until all homework was finished. But this led to Philippe lying and concealing and forgetting about his homework (and Simone interrogating and reprimanding), so she changed it to no screens between 4 and 5:30 p.m. But this led into terrible tangles over enforcement. Philippe would sneak screen time shamelessly, and then argue for exemptions, attempt to make bargains and, when all else failed, engage in emotional theatrics. So everyone dreaded this regimen.

This pattern persisted into middle school and when Philippe was in the seventh grade, his parents decided to have him retested. This time, the conclusion was "definitive": ADHD. When the psychologist shared the diagnosis with Philippe, the boy's reaction was muted. He nodded as she explained what it meant, and he said that he understood. But afterward he was extremely angry. He first directed his anger at his parents for taking him to that "stupid doctor," then he directed it at the stupid doctor. Meanwhile, the best treatment was a matter of debate. While Simone was in favor of trying medication, Arturo was reluctant. This discussion over medication threatened to open a dangerous split between the parents, but in the end Philippe made it clear he wasn't about to take any "stupid pills."

The psychologist made a number of recommendations. These included accommodations for Philippe—being allowed to write exams in a private room with fewer distractions, for example, and suggestions for the teachers to check in with Philippe after they'd given verbal instructions to the class to ensure he understood what they expected of him. While the results seemed clear and the suggestions sensible, things at school didn't change much. Nor did the family's home life see much improvement, with Philippe continuing to do the minimum and Simone in constant overseer mode, keeping track of what was coming next. When exams did come, Philippe mumbled something to his parents about his "accommodation," but they later learned that he declined to take advantage of it and instead wrote his exams with his classmates. He was embarrassed about looking like a "spaz."

During the seventh and eighth grades, the boy's unruly conduct at home continued, and his relationship with his mom became more strained. He was aggravated with her "constant nagging" and felt, quite genuinely, that she had some kind of grudge against him. She never treated Julie that way. Philippe had developed a sour attitude around his family, and sometimes was an embarrassment to his parents when he was rude and disengaged in public. From time to time, the parents recalled the possible Oppositional Defiant Disorder diagnosis, and scratched their heads unhappily.

One night during Philippe's first year of high school, the family was at another home for dinner when Philippe's behavior became so provocative that Simone reacted and they had an ugly spat in front of everyone. Later, a friend pulled her aside and, after awkwardly beating about the bush, asked if she'd considered whether some of the family strife and "parenting issues" might have something to do with Philippe's problems. Biting back her angry, defensive response, Simone shifted the topic. But the next day she called me.

Special Needs in Childhood

One of the great advancements in our understanding of children's development is the ability to identify when a child's ability to take on the problems of the world has been compromised. When it comes to our cognitive and emotional makeup, we've all been dealt a unique hand. Some children are hardwired to have problems with learning, attention, social comprehension and emotional control. These kids struggle not only in the classroom, but also on soccer teams, at summer camp, even while playing in the park.

Knowing when children are less able to function in these areas means that we can help them keep pace with their peers while they catch up in their areas of weakness. It would be impossible to overstate how valuable an advance this has been. Take the identification of learning disorders (LD) as an example. In many ways the science is still in its infancy with little (but growing) consensus on how to differentiate the various disorders, but there's no doubt that some kids cannot learn at the rate we would expect, given how smart they are. This, in fact, is the essence of a learning disability: a discrete area of weakness (poor nonverbal reasoning abilities, for example, or relatively slow processing speed) that impairs a child's ability to make use of his or her other cognitive abilities.

Learning disabilities are immensely frustrating for children, who are generally smart enough to know when they're not getting stuff, often from a pretty early age. Without a more sophisticated way to understand their lack of success, it's easy for children with LD to generalize the weakness into a sense of being "stupid" or not as good as other kids in some way. And for many kids this painful notion is so uncomfortable that there is a natural aversion not only to those activities that expose their weakness but also to actually having to think about and acknowledge that the problem even exists.

By a certain age and stage, however, the identification of an LD often comes as a welcome relief to kids. By looking at their "profile"—the pattern of scores on tests showing areas of both strength and weakness—children can see the big picture and put their struggles in context. These kids aren't "stupid" at all, it turns out, and often even have above-average scores in some areas, but one darn thing keeps tripping them up. By looking at their school experience through this lens, we can usually help students understand exactly why certain things have seemed so difficult for them and this can be a real "Aha!" moment for them.

Some children, though—Philippe, for example—are so uncomfortable with their disability that they are unwilling to take the candid look required to benefit in this way. Still, a diagnosis is extremely helpful. With a more exact understanding of a child's strengths and weaknesses, teachers can modify their strategies and the curriculum to minimize the adverse effects of the disability. Accommodations such as access to a keyboard for certain assignments or more time to complete tests are now common in classrooms across North America.

Whenever we identify an LD or other emotional or intellectual challenges, perhaps the greatest benefit is helping adults better understand a child's conduct. Unaware of the real origins, people will often attribute bad behavior to whatever seems the most likely. When they see a kid who has trouble paying attention, has a lot of physical energy and is disruptive and unruly, they'll assume he has a bad attitude and lacks respect. But knowing that it's actually an expression of ADHD leads to more compassionate, understanding relationships between the child and the adults around him. In past ages adults lacked an understanding of these types of impediments to learning, and without this perspective, saw such children as lazy, good-for-nothing or even "bad seeds."

Learned Helplessness

Outside of his academic struggles and the family fights, Philippe was a happy and popular kid. But there was no doubt in my mind that he fit the ADHD diagnosis. We reviewed the reports from the two previous assessments and these, together with reports from school and Arturo and Simone's observations, painted a clear picture. Philippe had weak working-memory skills, had great difficulty planning and organizing his efforts, was highly distractable and, in many settings, had a hard time sitting still. One area where this really showed up at school was in his writing, where his organizational difficulties and tendency to get sidetracked put him at a real disadvantage. Because writing assignments were particularly unpleasant for him, he routinely avoided them or, when he had no choice, simply rushed through them. Interestingly, but not atypically, Arturo recognized many of these experiences from his own childhood and even from adulthood. An intelligent and successful businessman, he had long ago realized he needed to have an assistant manage many details for him. "Well," he said wryly, "I'm pretty sure we know where Philippe gets it from."

No matter what Simone and Arturo did to try to help their son, they never saw any improvement in his organizational skills. They were frustrated. "He won't use the strategies we give him," his dad said. So they found themselves in power struggles with him and the blowups continued as Philippe raged at his parents when they asked him to do anything. He'd shout and swear and storm out of the room.

Still, they were shocked when the school called to warn that Philippe was in danger of failing a course. As bad as things had been, they'd never been this dire. Simone and Arturo asked for a clear list of the assignments and worked to keep Philippe on track. But this was a stressful and fractious job. Philippe often complained bitterly about school and how unfair things were. Simone could cajole him into sitting down to his homework, but he would rush through it and then more or less quit as soon as she turned her back. When he missed a critical assignment, his solution was to drop the course even though the principal had explained the consequences: Philippe would be going to summer school.

We weren't sure how much of this was because of what Philippe couldn't do (or, rather, was weak at doing) and how much was because of what he wouldn't do (or, rather, avoided). Simone and Arturo saw how Philippe's ADHD hampered his efforts at school, but what accounted for this worrying avoidance? Didn't he get that school was important?

As we have seen, parenting is a tightrope walk: we must make sure that we are available and supportive, ready to step in and assist when necessary, but also leave our children on their own with their problems enough to learn how to cope with them.

This is true for all children, even those with special needs such as ADHD.

Still, when your kid has a special need, you must err on the side of support more than you otherwise would. Philippe had needed his mom to follow behind him and quietly organize things for him more than others might have needed, and he had required more support with his academic efforts because these were areas where he wasn't operating on a level playing field with other kids. By making these accommodations, Simone and Arturo were able to set Philippe up for greater social and school success. And this certainly helped him to adjust to a context (school) that he was not ideally suited for. And in many ways it had paid off: he was a generally happy kid, popular with his friends, a nuisance to teachers but not at all unlikable, and still hanging in there academically.

Nevertheless, a parent in this position must also find a way to step out of the helping role enough to allow a child to develop some of his own coping skills. And, more important, his own relationship with the problem. Simone and Arturo had unintentionally assumed a level of responsibility for Philippe's success that had left their son increasingly in the passenger role, a role he was only too happy to occupy. We agreed: we needed to get Philippe driving the bus.

Habitual reliance on parents to take care of unpleasant tasks provides the perfect conditions for learned helplessness. Kids in this position are invested in their helplessness, and Philippe had little interest in getting things on track at school. In an attempt to merely support him while he learned to cope on his own, Simone started to feel she was indispensable to him: without her intervention, supervision and constant attention, it seemed, he wouldn't be able to function at all.

Philippe was another child stuck in first world thinking. He battled his parents rather than dealing directly with reality and he blamed his folks for the hardship in his life rather than accepting that hardship is actually part of life. In his resistance to school, he had chosen to avoid thinking about his actual weaknesses, his ADHD. To live in denial like this, he had to take on his parents, because they weren't in denial and they continually tried to push reality under his nose. That meant he was in a seemingly constant struggle for control with them, but this solution seemed preferable to the alternative: dealing with his problems. To the extent it worked, the payoff was that he could stay comfortably in the first world: appease his parents and otherwise stay under the radar and have fun.

While an assessor might suggest Philippe had Oppositional Defiant Disorder, such a diagnosis would be unfair because it attempts to locate the problem in Philippe—he is oppositional and he is defiant, and these are disorders. In this case, though, these issues are actually systemic: they exist in the relationship between parents and child, or more accurately in the triangular relationship of parents–school–child. Understanding that Philippe's avoidance is part of a larger problem—his parents are holding the worry ball too firmly, for example—is essential to finding a solution. Naming it a disorder in the child takes us in entirely the wrong direction.

Illnesses, Disorders and Labels

The Diagnostic and Statistical Manual for Mental Disorders, IV-TR (DSM, 4-TR) is the book that lists diagnoses such as ADHD and ODD. It is a manual published by the American Psychiatric Association and, as the 4-TR indicates, it's continually being revised and reissued in order to stay abreast of advancements in our understanding of mental functioning, and, increasingly over the last 10 or 15 years, advances in brain science.

For Simone and Arturo, learning about this book and how it worked was helpful in understanding Philippe's ADHD more accurately. Most people have heard of many of the disorders listed in the manual (depression, bipolar, autism, ADHD and so on) because these are household words these days. But there is widespread misunderstanding of what the terms actually mean—and what they don't mean.

For starters, it's important to realize that the disorders listed in the book are "syndromes," collections of symptoms that are clustered together because they tend to show up together. While the DSM does include information on what can contribute to these difficulties, the syndromes themselves are not based on an understanding of the pathogenic cause, as is the case with an "illness." The manual represents our best efforts to carve the mental illness pie into discrete areas of difficulty, based on the different ways people seem to suffer. And because our science keeps developing, every few years we need to reshuffle the deck, dropping old diagnoses and adding new ones. It's instructive to know, for example, that homosexuality was listed in the DSM as a disorder until 1974.

We are now waiting for the release of the fifth version, which has been postponed because of a lack of consensus among the psychiatrists and psychologists in charge over how to organize and conceptualize some of the disorders. When it does come out, the new version will include important changes. For example, the breakdown of learning disorders—understanding the different ways people can be learning disordered—should be much better. The current version is extremely simplistic in this regard: it lists three different disorders, one each for reading, writing and arithmetic, thereby following a classification system based on curriculum requirements rather than an understanding of compromised cognitive functions. But we now know a great deal about these functions. A diagnosis such as Nonverbal Learning Disability (NLD), for example, will no doubt be listed and this will greatly advance our work with children who struggle with this weakness. But, we have to realize that when the DSM-VI comes along (whenever that is), things will be reshuffled once again.

This is not to say that the diagnoses listed in the DSM are without value. Far from it. In fact, they are a scientific and clinical necessity. But it's important not to mistake these syndromes for illnesses in the causal sense. The conceptual error of doing so is more obvious with some labels than others. Labeling children like Philippe as having Oppositional Defiant Disorder, as if he has some specific malady that is causing him to act that way, is just intuitively wrong. Many psychologists and psychiatrists are hoping that ODD is omitted from the next DSM. Or at least I am. Almost always, the label is used as a fancy way of saying "pain-in-the-ass disorder." The point is, thinking so concretely about any of the syndromes in the manual is at least somewhat misleading and unhelpful.

For Simone, a pharmacist who naturally thought about the world in literal and causal terms, it was particularly easy to view Philippe's ADHD in this concrete way: he had ADHD, a "medical" diagnosis and therefore an illness, which caused certain behavior problems. These could be treated (medicine was available, for example), and accommodations could be made at both the parent and teacher level. This model, which I'm suggesting Simone operated by at an implicit, unstated level, places the patient (Philippe) in an entirely passive position: he suffers from the illness, which acts upon him in pathogenic ways. While the wrongheadedness of this thinking may seem slight, the truth is it omits something critical: the extent to which Philippe's behavior is not explainable by way of ADHD. At a certain point, his poor effort at school is surely just that: poor effort. It's not a question of whether he can't do the work or won't do the work, a lack of capacity or a lack of trying. It's not either/or; it's both/and. Philippe is both compromised in his ability and, by the time he saw me, invested in not trying.

This is what's tricky, and important to remember, about all of our current diagnoses in psychology and psychiatry. Depression, anxiety, attention deficits—these are all real difficulties for people, and these words identify truly different ways they suffer and struggle. In many cases these difficulties have a biological origin; Philippe's difficulties in school were reminiscent of his dad's, for example. But in each case, the way they express themselves are deeply related to an individual's experiences in the social and familial world he grew up in. None of the disorders in the DSM have any true type because there is tremendous variability in the ways people express these problems. As a result, under each disorder in the manual, there are always attempts to sort through the various subtypes, and then, because it's not possible to cover everything, under each disorder there is the catchall "NOS: Not Otherwise Specified."

Arturo may have had the same predisposition for ADHD, but he didn't get in fights with his parents the way Philippe did, and he never fell behind at school or frustrated teachers to the extent his son did. But then again he grew up in an entirely different era, one in which students were genuinely fearful of getting in trouble at school, of not doing work, one in which parents had far more natural authority at home.

One of the ways to keep the DSM and its labels in proper perspective is to remember that many of the "symptoms" on which the labels are based (low mood, difficulty focusing, restlessness, fears about the future, trouble sleeping) are things almost all of us experience at some point in our life. In addition, there are few symptoms in the DSM that appear on only one list (related to only one condition), while most appear on many. So we are talking about difficulties that stem both from biological predispositions and from the challenges we all face in building lives for ourselves and managing our relationships in the world.

Understanding this altered the way Simone and Arturo thought about Philippe's ADHD in subtle but important ways. It allowed them to see that while he really was at a disadvantage with his ADHD, he also lived in far too much denial of his problems. Their son, they realized, didn't just suffer from ADHD, he suffered from a kind of emotional immaturity as well: a strong disinclination to acknowledge his difficulties and deal with them. From this perspective, convincing Philippe to become his own manager of his ADHD became as crucial as managing the ADHD itself, perhaps even more crucial.

Frontal Lobes

One of the things they didn't know about when they wrote the DSM-IV is the set of brain functions associated with the frontal lobe. These are called executive functions. Great strides in neuroscience have taught us about these diverse brain processes that relate to the planning and carrying out of organized behavior. Studies have demonstrated that the ability of the frontal lobe—the most human part of the brain, you might say—to carry out a number of important functions (planning, initiating and monitoring goal-directed actions, inhibiting inappropriate impulses and maintaining focused concentration) varies from person to person. These functions are critical to successfully adapting to the world around us. Although it is not a perfect metaphor, this part of the brain is similar to the conductor of an orchestra, while the rest of the brain is the orchestra. When people are weak in this area they are at a disadvantage when they have to organize and coordinate their own efforts.

It's not hard to see the connection between what the DSM-IV calls Attention Deficit Hyperactivity Disorder, a description based on externally observable behavior, and Executive Functioning Weaknesses, a description at the level of actual mental processes. But there remains considerable debate about how the two concepts overlap, and this is just one of the many conceptual knots the writers of the next DSM must work out.

Nor is it hard to see how Simone and Arturo, thoughtful, caring people operating in an age of obligated parents, fell into the role of surrogate frontal lobes: the executive functions Philippe was weak in (planning, organizing, anticipating challenges) are exactly what "over-parenters" do too much of in the first place. By the time he reached his first year of high school, Philippe was accustomed to his parents operating as his frontal lobes, and they were having a hard time resigning from the position.

When, at my urging, they stepped back from managing his school responsibilities, he immediately failed, thus appearing genuinely unable to handle things on his own. Without his parents supervising his homework, Philippe did none of it. When this led to last-minute scrambles to get assignments in, crises during which the boy complained loudly to his parents, they worked hard at saying as little as possible. When his complaints didn't spur them into action, he would spend a hasty 15 minutes scratching something out that was, even from his parents' distant vantage point, clearly inadequate.

He lacked resiliency, his parents noted. With little stick-to-it-iveness, he quickly packed it in at his first brush with frustration. One way to view this problem was through the lens of ADHD/Executive Functioning Weaknesses. People with these difficulties, whose internal conductors are weak at keeping the whole brain orchestra playing together on a common piece, who are easily distracted by other, more interesting internal ideas, have trouble staying with tasks whenever they encounter challenges. But the other way to understand this problem was as a reflection of emotional immaturity: Philippe lacked frustration tolerance in the way all children who don't want to grow up lack it: he was behind in accepting reality. Again, it's not one lens or the other; it's both. On top of his ADHD, Philippe was emotionally immature.

But Simone struggled with my advice, admitting that she was only half able to follow it; in fact, despite stepping back to some extent, she and Arturo acknowledged they still checked in with Philippe about homework, provided pep talks (Mom) and lectures (Dad). In some ways this was the worst possible approach for Philippe: his parents were still clearly emotionally caught up in his school responsibilities (and so keeping alive the old, first world parent–child system), but no longer providing the actual support he had benefitted from.

Perhaps inevitably, Philippe failed history. Because Simone and Arturo had stepped back—stopped insisting he do his homework in the kitchen, for example—they'd had no idea he'd even been struggling that much in the course. Nor did they realize he'd missed several assignments, including some he'd actually completed, but never handed in. And he'd never let on that he was falling behind; as he later explained, "I was worried about how you would react."

A first world comment if ever there was one.

Avoidance Disorder—Not Otherwise Specified

Until she was about 16 years old, Easha enjoyed an enviably blessed and happy life. A bright and attractive girl, she was also a gifted athlete and played soccer at the highest rep level. She and her parents had their sights set on an athletic scholarship at a prestigious Ivy League university. But toward the end of her third year of high school, the wheels suddenly came off.

Easha had been injured in the fall and unable to play soccer for several months. While this was disappointing, she later told me that she'd taken advantage of the injury to focus on her schoolwork because she was aware how important her marks for that year would be for gaining university admission. So her first semester grades were higher than usual, and as she headed into second semester, healing well from her injury, it seemed that all was smooth sailing.

But as the term went along, Easha had a harder and harder time keeping up with the work, especially compared to the academic standard she'd set in the fall. Once she started attending training sessions regularly after school, she had considerably less time for studying. At soccer too, things had changed. Out of the loop for so long, and out of shape relative to the other players, Easha now had to work extra hard to keep up, and to keep her place on the team. The sport started to become stressful in a way it never had been.

Just before the March break, Easha stayed home one day when she felt unprepared to take a math test. She'd studied the night before, but not long enough and not well enough in her view; her growing level of stress had made it too difficult to concentrate and she'd had a miserable night. Telling her parents she felt ill but not that she had a math test, Easha stayed in bed all day. The next day, she went to school but skipped math class to avoid an encounter with the teacher. This was the first time in her life she had skipped. She hid in the library, feeling wretched. Easha managed to make it to the end of the week and the relief of March break, but suddenly there was what seemed to her a big pile of problems awaiting her return. She dreaded the Monday after the holiday when she would have to go back to school and face her mounting pile of troubles. Easha didn't realize it at this point, but she was already hooked on avoidance.

Avoidance is a common response to anxiety. Guidance offices, especially at girls' private schools like the one Easha attended, are swamped with anxious teenagers who are stressed out, can't sleep and, in some cases, are about to collapse. In the past, kids likely had less anxiety. Was anxiety even a concern for kids in an agrarian culture with no notion of advancement, or even of leaving town? Probably not. More likely, children in ages past grew up with a lot more fear—of injury, disease and animal attacks—and a lot less anxiety. So anxiety disorders have an inherent cultural context.

"Anxiety" is one of those words you will find in the DSM. Though we often use the term casually, it's also a technical word. (Similarly, depression is a technical term that many people now use in an everyday sense to mean "sad, in a prolonged or constant kind of way," which isn't actually far off from the DSM's definition—Not Otherwise Specified, of course).

I think most people see anxiety as a bad thing, something that you have more or less of; more is bad and a lot is so bad that it can lead to panic attacks or breakdowns. Among many young men, anxiety is also associated with weakness and is therefore somehow shameful.

In fact, anxiety is connected to our frontal lobes: it is always anticipatory. It's an emotional response to looking into the future and perceiving a threat. Ideally, this leads to an adaptive response as we use our frontal lobes to plan, initiate and carry out a solution while ignoring other inappropriate ideas and wishes, such as just ignoring the whole problem and hoping it goes away. And our ability to feel anxiety in this way and then to act on it is one of the things that really sets us apart from the rest of the animal kingdom. Consider, for example, how critical it was to human evolution that we started to get anxious about the winter and learned to cultivate and store food. Anxiety, when it leads to adaptation, is a good thing—and, in the right measure, an essential ingredient for flow.

But adaptive problem-solving is only one of the possible responses to anxiety. Avoidance is the other. Indeed, avoidance seems as hardwired a brain response as anxiety, so that I often wonder if we're actually not using two words to describe the same thing. Fear is linked to two different responses: fight or flight. Anxiety, which is basically fear plus planning, is linked in the same way: adapt or avoid. Sometimes I think what the kids I see are struggling with would be better described as an avoidance disorder.

Avoidance is addictive: the more you use it as a strategy, the more you have to use it. Most parents intuitively know this. So they use a little of their adult will at times to get their little ones to persevere and get out there—to convince their 6-year-old to go to soccer even though it's rainy and fun shows are on TV. Parents really do have to help kids avoid avoidance in the early years. Let your daughter skip dance too many times because a) she's whiney and b) you're too tired anyway, and this relaxed and stress-free approach can become a habit. So the lessons here aren't just for parents with kids with anxiety disorders, they are for all parents because all kids have some anxiety. Or, to put it the other way, many kids are inclined toward avoidance.

There are two kinds of avoidance: external and internal. External includes school refusal, skipping, not going to the party because of social awkwardness. Internal is avoiding thinking about whatever's connected to anxiety: seeking distractions (video games), chilling out (weed), rationalizing (hanging out with like-minded friends because if we're all doing it, it can't be that bad) or just plain denying (Philippe's response to the stupid doctor).

Monday morning after March break, Easha found herself unable to go to school. This time she didn't feign physical illness, she just came right out with it. She told her mother, Sheetal, how she was feeling: overwhelmed, unable to do it. "There's no point," she said in a defeated voice. Sheetal was struck by the depth of Easha's despair; the girl seemed genuinely distraught and she clearly believed that things were hopeless.

Easha's parents were second-generation Canadians, Hindus of East Indian descent. Both Sheetal and her husband, Rajan, were highly educated and devoted to their daughter, but they were at a loss about what to do. She refused to go to school that day no matter what. And insisting didn't seem quite right given how distressed and emotional she was. In the end, her mom talked her into going shopping for a new pair of soccer cleats in an effort to cheer her up. The next day, the parents managed to get her out of bed and off to school. It wasn't easy, but they did it. The next few months were turbulent and uncertain. Easha would manage to go to school for a few days, but then miss days at a time. Increasingly, she stayed in her room, often sleeping late or reading the fantasy books she loved so much. She generally went to school on days when there were soccer games, but soon she started to stay home and go to school only after classes were over and it was game time.

The change in their child—from studious and successful, to only half-functioning—in just three months, was terribly difficult for Rajan and Sheetal to understand, let alone deal with. This had certainly not been in their plans. When they received calls from the school asking where certain assignments were, Easha would become evasive, sometimes saying she had handed them in, or else saying that the teacher had been unclear about the assignment, thus raising doubts about it. One night, she faked an ankle injury to avoid going to soccer practice, and the parents knew it had gone far enough. She seemed to be slowly quitting life.

Easha was polite and extremely likable when I met her. She had a quiet, calm style and seemed to think carefully about what her parents and I said. She did not speak up much with her folks in the room, but privately with me she talked about her problems at school, saying they had just become too much for her. She spoke wistfully about soccer, saying she hoped to get back on track next fall. But she wasn't sure what to expect. She knew one thing for sure, getting as stressed as she was last year was not good for her—she was not going to ever do that again. She told me that she had adopted a new policy: if it caused stress, stop doing it. She believed her life was causing her to be stressed in a way that was actually harmful to her. She had to find a way to free herself from it.

"She seems like she's in Neverland," said her mother, alluding to the fantasy world of Peter Pan who never wanted to grow up. The degree of Easha's avoidance was disconcerting. Externally, she avoided school, avoided pulling her books out, avoided soccer practice; holed up in her room, she was largely avoiding the world outside her door. Internally, she avoided taking this problem on for herself; instead, she found ways to distract herself from her problems, escaping into the fictional world of her fantasy books.

Was this an anxiety disorder or an avoidance disorder? Did she have anxiety, Rajan and Sheetal asked me. Did she have depression? Well, maybe. She might meet the criteria for Anxiety Disorder NOS. Or was this avoidance? An avoidance disorder? Did it matter what we called it? Either way, the problem was the same: Easha had to stop avoiding. She had to take on the world and that would mean leaving the safe, if sometimes fractious, first world for the tense and stressful second world. She would have to accept setbacks and compromise her goals, not live in a fantasy.

Would medication help? Maybe, maybe not. Would she take it anyway? Maybe, maybe not. Important as these questions were, the questions around Easha's attitude toward the problem were just as essential. And she needed to be the person asking these good questions, not her parents. Once again, we were in a situation where the parents had to step back so the child could step forward and take responsibility for herself.

Suicide

Suicide is the most catastrophic failure. And since suicide is the second most common cause of death among Canadian teenagers, parental fears about it aren't entirely irrational. On the other hand, the far more common cause of death among teenagers is accidents, particularly car accidents. And most parents don't think twice about putting their children in their cars and racing them about to practices and play dates. So when parents worry about suicide, there are some distortions at work here.

Worries about suicide often linger at the edges of cases such as Easha's. In fact, it also seems to arise whenever parents are working to change things by stepping back and letting kids do some learning through painful failure. As we've seen, the situation so often has to get worse before it can get better. And it's usually at this point that many parents will say they fear that their child will just give up. Or perhaps they mean give in. It is a powerful fear and one that often makes it hard for parents to stay on the park bench.

It certainly was hard for Easha's parents. Although she had never made any reference to suicide and they never asked, they were worried about her, and so was I. She was a high achiever. Suicide is not easy; it takes real commitment in a way, and I had a feeling that Easha was the type who could pull it off, if she ever put her mind to it.

Although I did not believe that she did have her mind on it at that point, I met regularly with her parents, in addition to seeing Easha every week, and we agreed to keep a close, though quiet, eye out for warning signs.

Easha's mood was erratic. Sometimes she was irritable and dark and would retreat to her room, hunkering into her bed where she would bury her nose in her books. Communication with her at these times was nearly impossible—monosyllabic responses at best. She didn't seem down so much as remote, emotionally removed, uncaring. When she came back down to the first floor area (when she "returned," as Rajan put it), she could often be quite cheerful, as if there were nothing at all amiss in the world. Rajan had read that when your child goes through sudden mood changes, like going from being calm to being really happy or pretending to be happy, it could be a warning sign for suicide, so this cheerfulness did not put him or his wife entirely at ease.

Easha exhibited another warning sign they had read about: a growing disengagement from the world. Their observations showed them that, generally speaking, Easha's mood was not particularly low. Her steady state was actually a fairly satisfied equanimity. She occasionally fought with her younger brother, whom she loved to "parent" and boss around. She didn't exhibit many other important indicators of suicidal intent, such as frequently thinking or talking about death or dying, feelings of hopelessness, or overwhelming feelings of guilt or shame. Easha wasn't so much sad or distraught as she was hiding from the world within the safe confines of her family, bedroom and fantasy books.

Being present and paying attention to how Easha was feeling was critical to keeping her safe. By being aware of the dangers and staying observant, Rajan and Sheetal were able to protect her while giving her a chance to adapt to her situation. If she reached a point where she was at risk they wanted to know it. Despite the absence of any obvious "depression," the most significant of all precursors to suicide, I was seeing her regularly, so among the three of us we stayed vigilant.

Meanwhile, we looked at her predicament through the lens of her emotional development. Easha's had been a quite magical childhood up to this point. A lovely and intelligent child, in a close and loving family, she had experienced success in every aspect of her early life: school, sports, friends, even temple. She always managed to live up to the expectations of others because she was a "good" girl, willing to please, happy to accept the rules, knowing that this way everything was going to work out great. The please-and-appease world worked well for her, and without adjusting anything she was able to sustain her childhood fantasies: "One day I'm going to be an Ivy League soccer star." Then when reality started to hit, when the second world started to crash in around her, she suddenly had nowhere to stand.

It was fortunate that Easha's school had a good understanding of this type of problem. Its role was critical—and tricky. On the one hand, it had to find a way to set limits, and so a month into the new school year, when Easha had again fallen into a pattern of avoidance, the head of academics sat down with her in a private meeting and read her the riot act. On the other hand, it had to provide enough support and accommodation to coax the girl out of her defensive avoidance. To that end, the head of the school's learning center made an arrangement with her that, for starters, she just needed to come to school. She didn't have to go to class, she could just hang out in the learning center. And the school put a moratorium on tests and quizzes for her until she was attending class again.

How much of this was first world to second world adjustment and how much was an anxiety disorder she'd have to deal with over the long term was impossible to say. Once Easha had come to terms with her new reality and accepted its stresses and limitations, she might still be a relatively anxious person. Or a relatively avoidant person.

For her parents, understanding anxiety was important, but so was understanding how their daughter had to accept certain inconvenient truths of reality, including that she wouldn't be a scholarship athlete at an Ivy League college. She needed to leave behind the childhood version of ambition ("I'm going to be an astronaut when I grow up"), which was a world of fantasy, and enter the world of adult ambition, and the patient step-by-step progress it demands. Understanding this, they realized how important it was that they rein in their own fantasies about Easha (Rajan, especially, had shared Easha's belief that a golden future awaited her at Harvard, Princeton or Yale) and convey the quiet confidence Easha needed from them. She needed to know that they believed she would find her way, that struggles are normal, and that graduating high school and going on to the next step, whatever it may be, is all that matters. And they had to believe that this wouldn't seem too much for her.

In the end, Easha was unable to rise to the occasion at her private school. The offers of the staff in the learning center, the accommodations, the understanding and supportive approach were not enough, and she was unable to continue. A painful spring and summer followed, and the family had to endure almost another full year before Easha would be ready to go back to school.

A Happy Ending for Philippe

Philippe's school was willing to take on the responsibility of staying on top of him, but Simone fretted that he was "still not taking it seriously." She wondered if the school would "give up" on him. When she talked to Philippe about what he was going to do, she thought he seemed motivated to do better. But, though I didn't say it to her, I was certain that her talk with him had done about as much good as all her previous chats about using the strategies she'd given him. He likely seemed motivated because he knew that's how he had to look to appease his mother.

Simone and Arturo left my office resolved to really change their approach this time. And they did. Simone focused on getting a handle on her own feelings before engaging Philippe, and she and Arturo took a seat on the park bench. Arturo noticed when their son started tiptoeing around them: he offered full status updates regularly and reported on all his comings and goings. He was trying to get his parents to pick up the worry ball again.

They refused to pick it up. But they did pay close, sympathetic attention to his struggles with the worry ball and commiserated with him. After all, who doesn't feel a little overwhelmed at times? Soon, the family strife was rare and Philippe was spending more time with his parents in subtle ways, such as watching TV upstairs with them instead of in the basement by himself. And Simone and Arturo were devoting less time to talking anxiously about their son. "Now I'm focused on positive stuff, not on negative stuff, and I'm finally seeing him for who he is as opposed to what I wanted him to be," Simone told me, after she finally accepted the minding role. "I see the person he is trying to become. And it feels a lot better."

After another bad test at school, Philippe had a bit of a meltdown in front of his mom and dad. But, following the protocol, they stayed calm and reassured him that he would work it all out. Arturo even shared some tales of his screw-ups as an undiagnosed ADHD kid.

Meanwhile, once Simone put down the medication worry ball, Philippe picked it up. The day after his breakdown, he said, "Can you call the doctor?" Not stupid now. He added, referring to the medication for ADHD, "But I get to decide if I wanna keep taking them. I'm in charge of them."

"Yup," said his mom and dad. "You and the doctor."

DO keep an eye out for problems

Children require us to pay attention for many reasons, including so that when they really are in trouble—when they need special support or accommodations—we notice and take care of things. If a child has a learning disability, specific activities and tasks will be more challenging than they are for most other kids. If your child is struggling in school, watch for what's particularly frustrating or challenging. It's true that our children must learn to deal with the frustration of learning and keep at things, so avoid feeding into the complaining too much, but be sympathetic and keep an eye on things. It may be that school is especially hard in some way. By keeping a close eye, you and the school can make sure your child isn't at an unfair disadvantage. If that's the case, or if the school suspects it's the case, an assessment will help clarify things and allow the school to modify the child's program accordingly.

Paying attention for signs that your child is struggling with things emotionally is essential too. For almost all of us, there are periods of childhood when things aren't going well, when they can even start to seem hopeless or unbearable, if only for a short time. Being open to what your child is actually feeling, as opposed to what you think he should or shouldn't be feeling (harder than it sounds), will mean you'll know when he needs your support.

Occasionally, things can get terribly dark for children. If you know your child is struggling you will want to pay attention for signs that she needs you to be especially aware and helpful. Anxiety can sometimes get the upper hand with children in ways that are extremely difficult for them to handle, so children reporting desperate or panicky feelings about performance indicators such as marks, or personal achievement in sports; or demonstrating an unhealthy perfectionism, or an excessive or increasing reliance on avoidance are some of the things that will tell you he or she needs some emotional support. This may mean getting some outside help.

When children start to feel defeated or hopeless, when depression looms, they may tell you about it, and then it's really important to be open and ready to listen. But they may not talk, so if your child is withdrawing from friends and activities, or spending increasing hours on her own or in bed, or if she seems to not be enjoying things anymore, you will want to stay close by and let her know you want to help.

The most serious signs concern suicide, something that should be on our radar if we know a child is suffering from depression or excessive anxiety. Watch for talk about death and dying, reports of feeling hopeless, and self-harming behavior.

Of course, none of these are complete lists. The main thing is to be mindful: paying attention and being ready to step in when necessary. If you do suspect your child is trying to cope with a learning disability or an emotional problem, you will want to talk with her teachers and other important people in her life, and make a plan for giving her the support she needs.

Eight

Building a Village

Imagine you're at the park with your young son. It's a lovely day and you're sitting on a bench watching him play in the sandbox, just enjoying the scene. You're not 100 percent relaxed, though, because you didn't anticipate sandbox play and you've forgotten to bring along a little pail and shovel, like the parent of the lucky girl playing next to your boy. You can see how badly he wants her shovel, but she won't give it to him. Eventually, he bonks her on the head and takes it by force. She erupts in tears, naturally. When her mom sees this, she yanks the shovel out of your child's hand and gives it back to the aggrieved little girl. "What are you doing?" she asks him sternly. "You can't just take her shovel. Look, you've made her cry." Now your child starts to cry.

What happens next? A generation or two ago, this scene might well have ended right there. But not in the Age of Entitlement. Most parents these days would take some action. Not to do so would feel neglectful—or at least look neglectful to other parents (which might be worse). Not only do we have a strong impulse for protectiveness—that "Hey, what are you doing yelling at my kid?" feeling—but we're also highly aware that our child has misbehaved and most of us can't help but jump out of our seats and into the middle of the situation. "What are you doing?," we demand of the boy. "You know that's not okay. If you do that, we won't be able to come to the park."

But what do children learn if Mom or Dad always wades in like this? It actually distracts them from the world they're interacting with—where they're learning that people get really upset when you bonk someone on the head and take her shovel, which is an actual natural consequence—and puts it back on a parent who wasn't involved in the first place, but is now threatening natural consequences. They learn: "When I screw up in the world, Mom gets mad. If I can manage Mom's anger, I get to stay at the park."

Lost is the opportunity for learning about actual consequences (and gaining a greater respect for reality). Instead, a potential power struggle ensues: the next time he bonks someone on the head, the child will battle the parent over whether he gets to stay at the park. It becomes partly the parent's problem.

That's the risk of intervening here. When parents accept this level of responsibility, they become the custodians of reality for the child. Because they believe they are responsible for teaching the child about the world and administering justice, they increasingly become the ones responsible for managing his or her affairs in the world. It's a dangerous precedent.

This family dynamic is increasingly familiar to educators and mental health professionals: stressed-out parents trying to get their children to pay attention to their responsibilities; kids who seem distressingly out of touch with reality and whose biggest problem—in their view—is their "nagging" parents.

When I discuss the sandbox scenario with groups of parents and ask them to put themselves in the place of the parent who forgot the shovel and pail, people's reactions are quite fascinating. Usually, they feel at least one of two emotions: guilty responsibility and protective anger. And they feel quite strongly about it. The way the guilty responsibility people express it varies. Some think, "Oh, that poor kid, I bet Sally's mom is angry! I must apologize." For others, the first response is to re-parent, to get right in there and basically repeat what the first adult has already said. This is, in fact, by far the most common reaction these days. A common sentiment is: "I'd make sure my kid understands that that is simply not okay." And there are some really honest parents who admit, "I'd feel everyone was looking at me so I'd probably get even more angry at my child because he's embarrassed me." As different as these responses are, they all reflect the same sense of personal responsibility, or to put it the other way, a lack of a sense of separateness between child and parent. They are over-identifying with their kids.

The other responses—the angry, protective ones—range as well. Some parents react to my dramatization of the cross, admonishing parent: the strong words and angry tone are so harsh or frightening that they seem inappropriate. Others say they would first speak to the other parent—saying firmly, "I've got this"—and then turn and address the child (re-parenting, in other words). And some straightforward parents will simply declare: "It's my job, not yours."

But one day when I asked a roomful of parents how they felt, a woman piped up, "Better coming from her than me." It took a moment of stunned silence to get over my irritation at her for stealing my thunder—this was supposed to be a great bit of wisdom I was teaching. But I really shouldn't have been surprised: this is old school thinking; in fact, it's pretty much the way our parents raised us. This particular woman's style even reminded me of those days of parenting, especially the relaxed set of her shoulders as she spoke. She had the calm and sensible demeanor of a parent not caught up in the societal madness.

"So how do you feel in that moment?" I asked.

"Grateful," she said.

Hallelujah.

Here was a throwback to the days when parents who had teenagers hanging out in the park at night doing who-knows-what would say, "It's best that we don't know." Once that was standard; today it's immoral. Parents are not allowed to say that because it's far too unsafe. Most people need to be supported by a village to feel safe enough to say such things and, these days, too often the "village" is just not there.

The Tree Fort

Perhaps the greatest bit of good fortune in my childhood was the opportunity I had every summer to go up to our cottage on a large Georgian Bay island we shared with my extended family. I spent July and August there without interruption, my days filled mainly with exploring the island with my cousins Doug and Mike. Our activities included catching frogs, searching in garbage dumps for old beer bottles because they were worth five cents a piece and, most of all, building forts.

There had once been a hotel on the island my grandfather bought in the 1930s, and among its various ruins and garbage dumps were all manner of building materials for the determined fort builder. We'd watched our older siblings building forts and, early on, they excluded us from their activities, but eventually, after a few small developments on our own, they allowed us to join in. Finally, we were part of the building of The Tree Fort, an enduring testament to adolescent engineering that, 40 years later, remains a must-see destination on island walks.

A friend took a picture of The Tree Fort this past summer and I was struck by what it represented: an entirely child-created structure, built by kids, for kids, located in a forest 15 minutes' walk from the nearest house. The fort itself is in an impressive pine tree; on one side there's a solid granite outcrop 20 feet below; on the other side, the forest floor is 25 feet down. We carried up rotting lumber from buildings erected in the 1920s and nailed them to trees, started to build rooms, decks and even a lookout that was another perilous 15 feet higher (I didn't dare ascend to it for several years).

No parent, as far as I can recall, ever checked on the engineering of The Tree Fort. From early on, they would pass by on their own walks to admire it, but I don't think any of them ever climbed up to take a closer look.

Here's the thing: I was able to build and play in The Tree Fort. And I know how good an experience it was for me, and that we all survived, regardless of the risks. And yet, I would never allow my own kids to do this. I'm a pretty relaxed, permissive parent, but let my kids use sharp tools and push long boards around, way up in a tree 20 feet above solid granite with absolutely no supervision? Starting at age 10? I don't think so.

What's happened here? Am I a wimp?

Again, I don't think so. Or maybe I am, but if I am, then we're all wimps. Something has changed. Children do fall out of trees, and they do meet with accidents (particularly when not supervised by adults), accidents that can even prove fatal. As a society, we have decided to eliminate these accidents at any cost, and the cultural shift toward protecting children has been strong enough to trump my own experience. Rather than allow my kids to do what I enjoyed so much and grew so much from,

I prefer to err on the side of safety. And I do so immediately and unquestioningly. I mean, I would never let my kids do that.

I think this shift is fine and necessary. But I also now realize we have to think about the costs of this risk-averse, protective mentality. The more we protect ourselves, preserve our health and conserve our life (all practices based on future-based, anticipatory reasoning, which is the engine of anxiety), the more addicted we become to this strategy. At some point we're going to have to draw the line. We're going to have to say: okay, even though we could prevent it—the failure, the injury and some day, yes, even the death—we won't, because it's better for children's development to be at risk sometimes. We ought to face this terribly politically incorrect fact.

The Ingredients of a Village

Once, when we were coming home by boat from a new fort creation called "The A-Frame," Doug, Mike and I, aged 12 or 13, engaged in some risky and plainly stupid boat driving, swerving dangerously and freaking out Doug's mom, my Aunt Julie, who was watching from the front porch of my own family cottage. As we landed at my dock, still laughing hysterically, Aunt Julie hit us like a thundercloud: "What do you think you're doing? Don't you ever let me see you doing that again, or none of you will touch a boat the rest of this summer!"

Her rage was astonishing, her threat utterly convincing. From three giggling, carefree boys, we instantly became mute. And terrified. No boat? That was unthinkable. That was it for that day, no goodbyes, nothing. Doug slipped off quietly behind his mother as they headed to their cottage. Mike drove his boat—at a sedate half-speed—back to his cottage. I probably hid.

In a village, one parent can speak for another. Aunt Julie could "threaten" me with the loss of my boat and, for me, it was real. Parenting in a village is a shared responsibility among all the adults. Aunt Julie spoke to all three of us. And while she may have given something extra to Doug on their long walk home, on the dock, when she was yelling at us, she was definitely yelling at all three of us.

My great fortune to have had these experiences in a clan setting taught me something else as well: the tremendous value of being part of a social group that consisted of a range of ages. I was only in the first or second grade when my eldest cousin Bill started The Tree Fort. His building exploits soon became a legend for us youngsters. By the time we got on the tree (I established a "deck" perched precariously out over the granite), Bill was long gone. The upper floors and better chambers of the fort now belonged to a middle group of cousins who had taken over and somewhat grudgingly allowed us to occupy various fringe locations.

It's hard to imagine a better training for life in the real world. Talk about learning to climb the ladder. We stayed out of the way when necessary, and curried favor where possible (nails were always in short supply). While it was sometimes frustrating, it was incredibly engaging too. We had serious flow.

There was an implicit caring function in the relationships between the older and younger kids. We were allowed on the tree, truly, out of a sense of obligation. If we got hurt, the older kids ultimately had to make sure we got home to a parent. Our older siblings didn't particularly want us there so we knew we were there on sufferance. But sometimes we were friends too. And on special occasions, the whole clan—including members from many decades—gathered. Now when we're on the island with my own kids, I see this continuing, with older children looking after the young. This sharing of parenting duties helps everyone, parents and children alike. In villages, the parenting function is effectively shared, and this makes all the difference.

Compare this with our children's lives: as they become increasingly programmed and safeguarded, their social worlds are increasingly restricted to peers of the same age. They are with younger and older children far less often and unless they are volunteering or working in official adult-sanctioned and supervised positions, they are almost never responsible for other kids. This means they lack the experience of being cared for by older children and the experience of caring for younger ones. So implicitly they learn: "I am the child and the parent is the parent. Always." This is something that only deepens the child's sense of entitlement to being cared for, and the parents' sense of obligation to do so. And deepens the gulf between child and adult—increasingly, two utterly distinct things—leaving more and more children uncertain how they will ever get across the great divide.

To build a village, we have to accept that any adult has permission to parent. In a village, everyone—children and adults—understands that the parenting role is a shared one. We want our fellow adults to feel that their authority and, when necessary, their strong disapproval is what we want from them. Too often these days it's the other way around: we feel as though we are picking up another person's fine china when dealing with other people's kids.

Maybe it was my experience growing up in the village I had on the family island that led me to be an adult who's willing to speak up. For the past 10 years, I've worked in a Toronto neighborhood that's known as the gay village (which, coincidentally, is another community forged from a need to band together and look after each other). One day, as I was coming out of the local coffee shop, a line of preschoolers was making its way down the street. The kids clutched a rope in pairs, with their two weary early childhood educators at either end. They were impossible to miss because they'd taken it into their heads to scream at their high-pitched loudest. As a group. It was remarkable how obnoxious it was; people across the street were turning their heads in shock and discomfort.

Time for a little village parenting, don't you think? I did. As I caught up with the line and was parallel to the last of the shriekers, I suddenly yelled at them: "Stop it! That's not okay!" I mean, I really yelled, using my absolutely-not-okay father voice. On a major downtown street, in the middle of a workday. The line of children jerked to a frightened halt and I briefly caught the sight of a dozen stunned little pairs of eyes as I quickly nodded in what I hoped was a supportive, only-too-happy-to-help way to the young woman at the front of the line. I'm not sure my brief reassuring look was enough to overcome her obvious alarm, and I'll never know because I just kept walking.

But I took great satisfaction in the silence I left behind me.

Us Against Them

The ingredients of a village—trust among adults, gatherings and relationships that include several generations and various ages within them, and a sense of collective responsibility for the young—are becoming ever harder to find. This was especially true in the case of Kevin because his parents both came from other places, his mother from the United States and his father from rural Manitoba.

When I met him, Kevin was just turning 18 and was three months from graduating. Intelligent and athletic, he was accustomed to good grades and generally doing well at school. Still, he preferred "gym and recess," the oft-heard boy response to "what are your favorite parts of school?" In the seventh grade, his parents sent him to a private school in another part of town and though he protested that he wanted to stay with his neighborhood friends, he actually liked the school for the first couple of years. By the ninth grade, though, he was claiming that his parents "forced" him to stay there. Throughout high school, he did the minimal amount of work required (which was fairly little) to maintain a mid-70s average. Nevertheless, his marks at the time of his graduation from high school were good enough for most Canadian universities and he had provisionally accepted an offer from a university out of town. He just needed to keep his marks above 70. When I met him, Kevin had not been to school for three weeks, was falling further and further behind in his courses and suddenly that minimum average was in jeopardy.

His parents, Scott and Linda, had separated a year and a half earlier, but it was as amicable as these things can be so there was no evident hostility between them, just a faint frostiness. Linda opened our meeting by saying, "Kevin hates school and has for years." A self-admitted "nag," she described him as "very bright" and admitted that she and Scott pressured him to keep working, but he responded by saying he felt sick or had a headache. Her two concerns beyond his work ethic were that he spent way too much time online and that he wasn't as happy and outgoing as he used to be. Scott also thought the boy was too quiet and worried about his unhappy attitude toward school.

Although he said little while his parents were in the room, Kevin told me he was having trouble sleeping and this was affecting his schoolwork. He noted that his parents were "on his back" and gave as an example his mom's nagging about driving lessons. Despite pressure to spend more time at his dad's, Kevin didn't like to go there because all his father did was ask him about school and complain about how much time he spent gaming online. He also complained that when his mom was upset with him, she called Scott, who would come over and play the heavy. "Every time I see him he just gets on me: 'You have to work hard, get good grades, get the degree, get the money. . . .'"

Kevin was certainly a disengaged teenager; in fact, it radiated out of his pores. He complained that his dad didn't play with him more when he was younger and now that his dad wanted to spend time with him, Kevin's attitude was: "You missed the time when I wanted to do stuff with you." He dismissed his teachers as idiots and considered the work at school completely irrelevant. He was a nice kid, with a pleasant, friendly energy, but I found his unwitting sense of entitlement off-putting.

His talk was so full of blame that his perspective seemed to omit all sense of personal responsibility for his own fate, implicitly leaving this to the adults ("My mom always thinks schoolwork has to be done right away; it's so irritating"). When he argued with his parents in front of me, he stated emphatically that he did do things other than play video games: "bike riding," for example, and "shopping." He had no awareness that he needed to do some other things too—like contribute, work at something, have a life. His happy submersion in this blissful world of childhood was quite striking. With no inclination to attend to the demands of reality (school, his part-time job, a regular sleep cycle), he happily left the worrying to his parents, did the absolute minimum and frequently exploded at his mother for nagging and bothering him. This combination of expecting his mom to do everything for him and blaming her (often angrily) went to absurd lengths. An example: he raged at her for not waking him so he could accompany a friend to an important skateboard competition—it was 2:00 in the afternoon. But the times that Linda did wake him, he was often rude and uncooperative.

He liked to label his difficulties as a "sleep problem." He couldn't fall asleep at night, so he'd get up and watch TV or play games online until the wee hours of the morning. After a few sessions with me, I proposed he look at his problems through an anxiety and avoidance lens. Kevin acknowledged that he was worried about looking like an idiot at school, and that he agonized about what his friends would say when he suddenly started going again, and that when he thought of how much work he had to do, because there was now so much, he felt overwhelmed. But when we talked about this he looked beyond defeated—crushed and listless. Perhaps not surprisingly, he missed our next session.

Socially, he had a group of neighborhood pals he'd known since childhood, but they attended the local high school so Kevin lived in constant anticipation of the next time he would get to hang with them. Whenever he couldn't, whatever the actual reason, Kevin at some level went back to the fact that it was his parents' fault that he went to another school. Whenever he did get together with his friends, they still played very much like boys: biking, gaming and messing around. There wasn't much hint of sexuality yet and he wasn't that interested in girls anyway. Nor did he appear interested in exploring alcohol or weed. In both his interests and his orientation to the outside world, he was immature, preferring the carefree frolic of childhood to the overwhelming demands of the adult world.

In Kevin's case, this now-familiar situation was exacerbated by parents who weren't fitting into the world around them so well either. Scott and Linda's relationship with the school staff and Kevin's teachers was respectful, but strained. Linda kept a careful eye on their work with her son and she worried whether they would "follow through" on their "promises" (the school's plans for how to deal with the problem). She was suspicious about the teachers really having Kevin's best interests at heart and was occasionally critical, claiming they were unsupportive. Scott mainly deferred to Linda on these matters, but he was certainly worried (there was some truth to Kevin's complaints that his father harangued him about school whenever he saw him). Though they were engaged in their own blame game, Scott and Linda also felt guilty that they hadn't done a better job with their son.

All the weight of responsibility was on these parents and there was no one to back them up. I could even sense their wary vigilance of me: Would I really follow up with the school? At heart, did I really care? Did I just see them as another paying family? After all, I was not kin and not under any emotional or familial obligation. Their isolation was palpable.

They truly lacked a village. Linda's family, far away, was unavailable to them. Scott's family was also far away, but at least Kevin visited every summer. And he loved it there. From what he could tell from these visits, his cousins spent all their time engaged in outdoor activities such as riding ATVs and fishing, and his uncle managed a hockey rink. This last struck Kevin as one of the most amazing jobs ever, while his father Scott, in contrast, was clearly critical of his brother for not "making it."

I found it hard not to imagine Kevin in The Tree Fort. He would have been an awesome member, a great older cousin. He loved the outdoors, loved to play with kids of all ages. He probably would have gone up to the lookout on his first day. Some kids did. What if he'd grown up in his dad's village, hanging out at the hockey rink, ATVing, probably hunting, certainly ice fishing. Imagine how different it would have been for Kevin if, growing up at the rink and in the bush, he'd been surrounded by people of all ages, all of them important to him. Imagine if he'd seen his cousins during the school year too, saw them dealing with the stresses of the real world and saw them survive. Imagine his parents no longer at the center of everything.

But that was not Kevin's lot. His parents' isolation meant they held the worry ball especially tight. By the time their son had reached the end of high school, they felt completely responsible for overseeing his progress in the world, and Kevin exhibited an exactly-corresponding sense of entitlement to being taken care of. And avoidance. Kevin actually showed a lot of the features of an anxiety disorder—Anxiety Disorder NOS, I suppose. He relied heavily on avoidance as a strategy for managing his anxiety. And, as is typical, he used both internal and external avoidance strategies. External strategies are the obvious ones: not going to school, not making any attempt to do his homework, missing therapy sessions. The internal ones involve avoiding knowing about his problems, or recognizing them: labeling his problem a sleep disorder, for example, or blaming his parents for everything.

Safety Second

We are infecting our children with anxiety. All the protecting that Scott and Linda did was about anticipating problems. Even their choice to send him to a private school in another neighborhood at an early age was all about the future, about getting ahead. But it's easy to see how it happens. In the world they live in, a person's place must be worked for and earned. Nothing wrong with that, but it's also a world in which you must fight for yours because no one is going to give you any handouts. The underbelly of the American Dream and the cult of the individual is this "looking out for Number One" mentality. Whatever other evils we might want to lay at this doorstep, this worldview is surely one that is stressing the hell out of the next generation. Scott's unspoken message to Kevin is: "You can't stay in your village if you want to do anything with your life and your uncle is a loser for staying there. You have to have a plan, get out of there, don't fall behind, compete, find money." High schools reinforce this message, especially now that they start talking to students about university earlier and more earnestly than ever before (though, of course, they largely do this because parents want them to). "Plan ahead!" says the system. Start thinking about what you want to be. Should you focus on sciences in the upper high-school grades to go in the direction of engineering or medicine, or focus on the humanities, which might lead to law or journalism? But you have to start thinking about it in the first year of high school. No wonder our kids are anxious.

"School refusal" is a new disorder (though it's not in the DSM). Recently, I called a colleague at Toronto East General Hospital because I was overrun with kids suffering with the problem. I hoped she might be able to take a referral. I didn't realize her hospital had a school refusal program—and an endless waiting list. It seems that when our kids aren't in the basement, smoking weed and playing *Call of Duty*, they're stressing out and developing anxiety disorders.

It's also an anxious age because of how risk averse we are. Our technology isn't helping either. Cell phones mean we can monitor our kids far more closely than ever, but is this virtual tether really a good thing? Just because we can track them, should we? We were raised on "Come home when the lights come on," and "It's better we don't know," and we survived. Most of us even thrived. And how many kids did you know who suffered from school refusal? Who'd even heard the term?

Risk aversion—a form of avoidance—is highly addictive. We know this at an individual level: the more we avoid, the more we are tempted to avoid. But it's true at the collective level as well: the more we exercise caution to preserve life and limb, the more anxious about preserving life and limb we become. I feel it now with my tree fort: I loved it as a kid, but 30 years later, as a parent, letting my own kids do that without supervision feels unquestionably wrong. Let's face it: tree forts have changed. Today, Dad goes to Home Depot and then does the building for his kids. But guess what? Because Dad built it, the kids have no experience climbing the tree or being careful when up high, and so the parents have to establish rules (no going out the window, no sitting where there is no barrier) and then closely supervise any play in the fort so they can enforce the rules ("I saw you go out the window; there will be no playing in the fort if you don't obey the rules"). The inevitable result of this cultural development—again, with its roots in the Enlightenment—will be a society of safe but boring people who are also bored.

Over-Caring

All our anxiety doesn't just damage our kids, it also often hurts our marriages. Couples need to have a life together or they become exhausted and resentful. Sadly, in Scott and Linda's case the strain had proven too great and they had divorced, which instantly increased their isolation. In the case of Gemma's parents from Chapter 6, Martin and Annie were able to shift their children's behavior partly by reconnecting with each other and devoting time and energy to their exclusive relationship (date night, for example). This shifting of family energies had done the kids a world of good, freeing them up to just live their kid lives.

For many parents I've met, the loss of closeness in the marital relationship means a shifting of emotional energy to other parts of their life where those needs can be met—this often means the children. But investing all that emotional energy in our children isn't always helpful. It can be burdensome too, weighing everything down and making things less fun. It's certainly true that many parents find they have more patience for their kids when they've dedicated a little less of their life and soul to them, and revolved their lives around their children a little less.

Warren and Monica came to me exhausted. Part of that was inevitable with three kids under 10, of course, but they made it worse with their pervasive sense of responsibility. They rarely went out because they'd be too worried about whether their youngest would get to sleep, and when they did go out, one of them usually tried to return home by 9 p.m. That didn't exactly make them a fun couple to be with—and they weren't having much fun either.

Monica felt so responsible that when her 7-year-old daughter, Rachel, wanted to invite her friend Maddy over for a play date on a Friday after school, she said no. Why? Because then she'd have to worry about dinner: would it be kid-friendly enough? (We all had a good laugh when she told this story because she'd been planning to prepare some kind of "oat thing" that night.) The stress of hosting her daughter's friend made her say no.

But she could, I suggested, decide that she didn't want to be that responsible. If Maddy ended up staying for dinner, she'd get to try the weird oat thing, and that would be that. (Who knows? Maybe the girl would even like oats.) Then Monica wouldn't have to stress, Rachel would get to enjoy a play date and Warren would have a happier wife and be happier because of it—in other words, everyone wins. This idea came as a revelation to Monica. "Yeah," she said. "I'd prefer that."

Parents who devote everything to their offspring are crankier with their children, and more resentful of both the kids and each other. And all that parental devotion is actually a burden on the kids—there's a lot more pressure on them when Mom and Dad have given everything to them and focused their lives on them.

Sharing the Load

Our anxiety is a self-centered, me-first impulse. Yes, of course, it extends deeply to the kids; after all, they are increasingly the only others in our world, as our kin have become less a part of our everyday lives and our villages have disappeared. So we are at great risk of failing to think collectively about the future, to be fueled by collective anxiety. In terms of the sociopolitical forces that shape our culture, greed continues to trump social consciousness. The American Dream—which now means every person has the right to the fun and lavish upper middle-class lifestyle presented in the media—is still at the center of our collective ideology. And it may be at this fundamental level that we have to rethink the way we live. Village or individual (or individual family)? I'm not by any means the first to identify this: it started with Alexis de Tocqueville's prophetic and brilliant *Democracy in America*. A contemporary of Rousseau's, he observed the great development of democracy in America and identified its likely Achilles's heel: the cult of the individual. Since then, many sociologists have focused on this troubling issue.

This problem is now coming home to roost at the level of our children's emotional development. With all the responsibility shouldered by two parents (and sometimes only one), with parents absorbed in their children, and with the big, impersonal world looming outside the family "great room" (where Mom is trying to supervise homework, so that her kids can get ahead and be okay in the future, able to get great rooms of their own), it's no wonder that everyone has really started to drive each other nuts. Surely we can do better than this; Rousseau and de Tocqueville would certainly have wanted us to.

For starters, what we all need—children and parents alike— is a good village. A place where the setting of limits isn't always the exclusive domain of the biological parents. A place where external authorities (teachers, coaches, even other parents) are entrusted to "lay down the law" when and where it's necessary. Above all, a place where children learn to appreciate the rules and expectations of society by interacting directly with it.

A village is also a place where children play in an organic and relatively unsupervised way—organic in the sense that village play is not under adult auspices, the rules and expectations pre-defined by adults. It develops on its own, rules are fluid, older and younger kids intermingle and, ideally, sort things out for themselves much of the time.

A village isn't just good for our kids, it's good for parent–child relationships. It frees up parents to take on the compassionate, supportive bystander role as their children explore and learn about the world, instead of having to feel in charge and respon-sible all the time. And isn't this the place we all really want to be? But for this to happen, we need to take a stand against our pow-erful sense of obligation and personal responsibility, and trust that by not actively intervening we are not failing our children.

Finding a village is especially challenging these days, as parenting has become not only a "skill," but also something increasingly done in the isolation of the family home. But it's not impossible. You don't actually need a physical place to have a village. You do need to develop trust with other adults in the community, especially other parents, teachers and coaches. And sometimes you have to take on that role for your fellow village members, as I did that day with the shrieking kids on the street by my office. That means trusting other adults to be stern or to play the disciplinarian with your child and feeling confident that when you don't intervene—when you allow another adult to discipline your child while you "do nothing"—no one will accuse you of parental neglect.

You'll know you're getting close when you're able to sit tight as your child gets a stern talking-to from another parent. You'll know you're there when, afterward, you can say, "Thanks for your help"—and really mean it.

DO make safety second

There is no comparing how much more cautious we are with our children than any previous human society has been. We protect children emotionally and physically from the moment they are born, and the more we learn about what harms us (and we learn more every day), the more we protect. To some extent, this is smart: it's good to be safe and to take precautionary measures. It's good to wear helmets, and to create safety standards to take proactive measures to avoid injury and death. But how far do we, as a society, want to take this policy?

Something gets lost when we err unfailingly on the side of safety, and deny, restrict or supervise children's play. It costs children a direct and real exchange with the world around them. Play that is unmediated by adults, with no one to consult or rely on, no watchful eye to evade, and no parent to complain to, brings children into a direct relationship with reality—with all its exciting possibilities, as well as all its challenges and risks.

DON'T neglect yourselves

In my initial meeting with families, some parents proudly make certain comments they shouldn't really be proud of. They are "devoted" to their children, their lives "revolve" around the children and "Everything is about the kids in our house." They'll even say, "We love them to death." Love them to death, indeed. When parents burden their children with this level of devotion, it's actually not fair to the kids because it means they have to please and appease their parents even more. In addition, giving that much to your kids often means not paying sufficient attention to your marriage. The 6-year-old still sleeping in his parents' bed is a perfect symbol of this predicament and how it is probably not really good for anybody. Failing to maintain and honor other interests—in your spouse or the outside world—greatly increases the difficulty of stepping back from your children's failures because you've made the pull to identify with them all the stronger. Kids benefit from loving and devoted parents, but they suffocate under parents who don't have their own lives as well.

DO allow other (trustworthy) adults to be angry with or discipline your child

A sense of guilty responsibility ("I'm the parent so it's my fault Johnny is behaving badly") is enough to motivate most of us to step in and parent our child—aggressively—when we see he has upset other adults or children. Equally strong for many parents is a sense of ownership of the parenting function, particularly when we see another adult disciplining or reprimanding our child ("Hey, that's my kid—back off"). But another adult's admonishment of your child, when it's warranted and within reasonable limits, is the best thing for him. He learns that a certain behavior is not countenanced by society and that bad things happen when he engages in it. Our sense of ownership over the parenting function is a symptom of our relatively village-less world, where parents increasingly feel on the hook for every aspect of their children's behavior. That's why supporting other adults to play this authoritative role with your children is one of the most important ways of creating the kind of "village" that is best for children.

Nine

Building an Adult

I seem to like parks. We've already looked at the importance of sitting on the park bench and enjoying the show, and *staying* on the bench and allowing other village adults to set limits with your child when necessary. But let's go back there because there's something else important that happens in parks and playgrounds every day; it's something that parents and other childcare providers do repeatedly, and generally do well. It's something I've mentioned before—the importance of knowing when to *under*-respond to a child's woes. The most familiar example is when your 3-year-old trips and goes down with a good hard *whump!*—hard enough to shock the system, but no big deal. So when the toddler turns to look up at you, ready to really cry, many parents will be responsive—"Oh, ouch"—but less than completely solicitous, knowing that if they show full-out concern, she *will* really cry. By downgrading their response, parents send the message, "Oh, yes, I see, that probably hurt, and I'm here. But you're okay, and you will be fine, it's just a scratch."

Chapter Nine

Why is this so important? It's not about the crying. It's because this is the message that helps your child emotionally suck it up, pick herself back up and keep going. From a parenting perspective this requires a special kind of attending, because it requires discerning what children actually require from you by carefully reading their cues. If they need a full-out hug, then that's what you give them, or if it's a time when they can use a simple pat and encouragement—"Ouch, that hurts"—then that's what you do. If you watch skilled early childhood educators—and they are experts at this—they know just when children need something extra (a bit more of a hug; a longer, warmer reassurance). They also know when children will benefit from what infant researcher Daniel Stern calls an "intentional misattunement," and downgrade their response just the right amount so the kids get what they need and then get right back to their important childhood business.

When you don't do this, and instead show full-out concern and leap to help, not only will a child cry a lot harder, but (much more important) he will learn that such moments are really bad and to avoid them in the future. You will have missed an opportunity to help him develop emotional resilience. The good news? There will be another opportunity just around the corner—after all, reality never gives up.

These dynamics are exactly the same in later years, including adolescence. Fifteen-year-old Toby ignored his parents' reminders all weekend about his history essay, but on Sunday night he started to panic. His dad, Eric, sat down and reasoned with him: if he leaves things to the last minute like this, it's really not going to work out for him. So true, but how helpful was this finger-wagging to Toby? He had little to say to his dad, and later recruited Sarah, his mom, to help him scramble something together. She didn't say much but as they went up

224

to bed well after midnight, she couldn't resist a final editorial comment on the completed but clearly inadequate essay as "not being good enough." This didn't seem to do Toby much good either; he hung his head and seemed to shrink.

Imagine if Eric had responded sympathetically to Toby's crisis. "Sorry to hear it, Toby. You gonna be all right?" I wonder how Toby might have responded. I mean, after he got over his astonishment. And what if Sarah, equally sympathetic, had limited her helpfulness just a little—maybe going to bed at midnight, and letting Toby fend for himself from there. For one thing, she wouldn't have become so frustrated that she needed to make her negative comment. Over-reacting has the opposite effect of under-reacting: it makes the big world out there seem even more imposing and scary, and makes the child less inclined to pick himself up and keep going.

These trips and falls are an essential part of the process, not bad at all in the longer term, though certainly painful in the short term. And as kids get older they need different kinds of trips and falls; naturally, as they get older, they can take harder falls. This all-important stumbling process starts early in life. A 3-year-old can handle a good *whump* in the park, but when she was 8 months old she couldn't have. An 8-month-old, however, is already having 8-month-old trips and falls so that she'll be ready for the 3-year-old kind. Necessary painful experiences at 8 months include, for example, being startled by a sudden loud noise, or attempting to stand, not making it and falling painfully on a toy. At all of these moments, the competent parent downplays her response when it is appropriate: when the baby is startled by a dog's loud barking and looks at Mommy in fright, ready to cry, Mommy smiles and says, "Yes, that's a doggy."

Why do parents, who for the most part get this right in the early years, have so much trouble following this basic strategy later on?

First, they're too anxious about the consequences of failure and, second, they're too personally identified with their child's success.

This book has reported mainly success stories, but not all the families I've met have been so fortunate. Especially earlier in my career. But it's interesting to think about the non-successes. What happened to them? Did they meet with the catastrophic ending their parents feared? Teenage pregnancy? Drug addiction? Criminal record? Actually, no, that was never what defeated us. The kids just didn't leave home. Or, if they did, they soon ended up right back with their parents. They were "failures to launch"—kidults, adultescents. Safe and bored and at no risk at all.

Beware, parents. The real danger is not the catastrophes you are dreading, but just the opposite: risk-averse people whose lives lack engagement with reality—and flow.

Looking After Yourself

My friend's son, Tommy, who'd always been reasonably responsible about school, had a good time in the ninth grade playing *Call of Duty*. He delighted in rampaging through backyards and demolishing his friends with a machine gun. I can only imagine how I would have responded to this option in the heart of my capture-the-flag days: *Call of Duty* is like capture-the-flag with full visual effects. Because of this indulgence, by the time May came around and Tommy was facing exams for the first time in his life, he suddenly realized that he was slightly screwed. He resolved to work harder and his mom watched him struggle with the boring task of studying a textbook with the flaming glory of .COD just a keystroke away.

Studying in the ninth grade is hard. Studying in the ninth grade is really hard when you have an entirely safe but incredibly realistic warscape in which to battle your buddies, available to you at all times, right in your bedroom. It's like asking an alcoholic to stay sober in a bar. Tommy studied more, but not enough. June arrived, and he was in a panic. With exams just days away, he knew he wasn't prepared. He had to study; he'd reached the point where he couldn't play *any* more *COD*. So he asked his mom to "hide" his controllers. ("Lock the liquor cabinet, Mom.") She did and it worked well; unfortunately for Tommy, she went away before he could ask for them back, and he had some desperate days waiting to return to his backyard marauding.

As children encounter reality and learn to deal with it, their efforts will initially look, well, childish. But how else would they look? When required to deal with something difficult, kids will try whatever strategies occur to them; some will work better than others. I remember a video I saw in graduate school of 5-year-old children subjected to an almost cruel psychology "experiment": the kids sat at a table with a pile of yummy-looking jelly beans on it and the adult across the table explained that they could have the treats, but only after 10 minutes. Then the adult left the 5-year-old with the excruciating task of not eating one jelly bean. Entertainingly, as soon as the adult leaves the room, some children fail immediately. Others, however, struggle to keep their hands off, and their efforts seem to reveal their thinking. One girl memorably adopted the strategy of not looking at the jelly beans, but when this proved too difficult—she kept glancing at them—she turned her chair around to face the other way. Whatever works.

But in real life, parents do have to ask their children to tolerate difficult things, to ask them to look after themselves in some way. In fact, doing so is essential if they are to learn to take on the world for themselves. So when my friends Steve and

Lisa were struggling with their 4-year-old son Marcus's desire to climb into their bed in the early morning, they decided to do something about it. Getting mad at him wasn't working because he still came in and then they were all unhappy. So they made a rule: he wasn't allowed to come into their bedroom until 7 a.m. But Marcus was not adept at reading time, even on the new digital clock they bought him, and anyway he preferred to check in with Mom and Dad. So for a while he continued to leave his room, though he stopped entering theirs. Instead, he tapped on the door lightly and asked: "Are you happy? Or are you early?"

In our little community of families—a kind of village, I suppose—these now-famous questions have since become a sincere way of asking other people how they're doing: "Are you happy? Or are you early?"

From Child to Adult

It turns out what you should really be worrying about is helping your child become an adult, someone who is emotionally separate from her parents, who has her own relationship with the real world, a relationship characterized at times by anxiety, at times by boredom, but at other times by flow. This is what parents should worry about because it is the thing we are getting worse and worse at doing.

Needless to say, I'm not questioning the importance of lasting family ties and obligations. What I am talking about is that in order for children to become adults, they must take complete responsibility for their actions. One way to think about this process of going from child to adult, is as a shifting of responsibility from, at the beginning, total responsibility on the parent to, at

228

the end, total responsibility on the child. This is a gradual shift, with the child taking on more and more as the parent takes on less and less. The one cannot happen without the other.

We can plot this shift on a curve determined by the degree of responsibility appropriate for both parent and child at each age and stage. To my knowledge, no such ratios have ever been determined (if they ever could be), so plotting the points on the curve has to be approximate. I chose nine points (birth, 8 months, 18 months, 2½ years, 4 years, 8 years, 12 years, 16 years and 20 years), estimated the appropriate ratio for each point, and created the following curves:

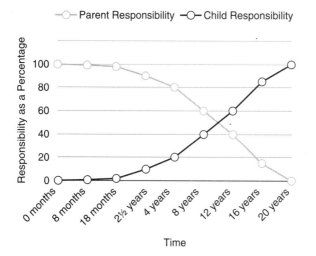

My parental curve, marking a relinquishing of responsibility, starts at 100 percent and stays well above 90 percent (all numbers obviously a little arbitrary) until well into a child's toddlerhood, and it stays well above 50 percent until he or she gets into the preteens. Somewhere around this point, though, things switch—or at least should switch—and the child begins to be more responsible for herself than the parents, until the time she is 20 and has taken 100 percent of the responsibility. Over this span, the parents are doing less and protecting less, so this is a curve of parental letting go. We can also think of the chart in worry-ball terms, with the ball fully in parental hands at the start, and fully in the child's by the end. In this sense the curve depicts a 20-year-long handoff of the worry ball.

The child's curve starts very low, but note: not at zero, even for the first two years of life. At 8 months, children can start to move around a bit, not necessarily crawling (though many do at this age) but at least squirming and reaching, so when a baby wants a toy just out of reach and begins to grunt and complain in frustration, competent parents will likely leave at least a second or two for her to decide to reach out and get it for herself, perhaps even encouraging her. The more the child does for herself, the more she must deal with the challenges of reality. So the mirror image of the parental letting-go curve is the child resiliency curve.

Let's call it the normal growth curve for resiliency, "normal" meaning it demarcates the ages, roughly, when the average child can handle what. Accommodation will have to be made for children with special needs, and their curve will look a little different, with the parental responsibility extending longer.

We all want to avoid having our child go through a crash course with reality, as many of the children I've described in this book had to. Not accustomed to enough painful disappointment and failure at earlier stages, they were unprepared for the kinds of failures that occurred in the later years. If we were to plot the curves of many of their families, we would see the parents' curve remaining quite high right into the teenage years, with the child's curve remaining correspondingly low. Then, when they get into high school, and reality really starts to set in, they are not prepared so we start to see avoidance and retreat to the first world, increasingly anxious parents *saying* to their child, "You've got to take more responsibility for yourself," but doing things (nagging, cajoling, threatening) that actually stunt a developing sense of responsibility.

Here is the crucial lesson: children need to be exposed to the appropriate level of hardship (and the pain and failure that goes along with it) all along the way. That is what builds emotional resiliency. You don't need to plan it—that would be weird. But you do have to relinquish responsibility every step of the way. Understand that as much as kids complain about parental nagging, many hate being responsible for themselves even more. So they won't take emotional responsibility unless they have to.

Once again, something parents get right in the early years seems to escape them in later years when, seemingly, the stakes are higher. In the early years, parents often act as if their child is *older* than he or she is. For example, all parents intuitively speak to their preverbal infants in full sentences, as if they could understand. And, lo and behold, eventually children can speak and understand. When we raise the bar on our children's competencies, *expecting* them to be able to do it, kids miraculously start to do it. Taking care not to over-react to a big *whump!* is the same thing; our response says, implicitly, "You can handle this."

It's a good illustration of how children take themselves—learn who they are—from what is in their parents' mind. When our kids crash in some way and we are not too freaked out as parents, but are emotionally available to them, they learn that we believe in them and support them and that these bumps and bruises are a normal part of the process. And this does them a world of good when it comes to building the confidence required to take on the big world out there.

Some Essential "Scraped Knees" of Childhood: When a Child Can Handle What

On the resiliency curve, I have the newborn infant at 0 percent responsible and the parents 100 percent. The newborn infant is actually able to do a great many things on her own; one of the most miraculous is breathing. Others include crying and sucking. All are important—essential, in fact—but all except for breathing are entirely useless if there's not another person around to respond. At this stage, the parent is entirely responsible for every facet of the child's life; she is responsible for nothing.

But it's never like this again. Growing up, from this one, narrow perspective, is a long slow process of relinquishing our claim on the parents who do so much for us, and accepting the inconvenient truths of reality. So imagine things eight months later: Mom is making dinner in the room next to the nursery as her baby has a nap. Mom hears the infant wake up because she's making small cooing noises as she gazes around from her crib. Suddenly, the tone changes, she calls out more loudly and unmistakably. Although the baby does not yet have words, Mom knows she is being summoned because there's an urgent "Where are you?" to her baby's cry that experience has taught her will soon turn into crying.

Eight months is a long time to get to know a person, and baby and Mom know each other pretty well at this point. So Mom knows she can finish getting the dinner out of the oven. Predictably, baby's voice rises and then begins to transition into a whining cry. Maybe she's about to start taking a big breath to really wail, or maybe she doesn't get that far. Because, suddenly, there's Mom and it's all okay. If she's left her too long, baby may well take longer to soothe, expressing a primitive anger at mother for failing her so. But Mom is calm, she disregards baby's angry "Where were you?" cry, and takes care of whatever needs taking care of smoothly, efficiently and, in a calm way, lovingly.

This is an early Story of Woe moment. Even at this age, parents must find ways to respond to their children's genuine hurts while not encouraging the tyrannical and controlling patterns that children can get into with parents who are too available and too anxious about failing them.

In this example, the baby is genuinely upset that Mom is not there, but she is also beginning to become intentional about her crying. She is developing an attachment strategy. And for the purposes of developing the child's confident expectation that things will be okay, it's so important for parents to be reliably responsive at this stage. By reliably responding to these cues, parents help children develop a secure attachment and the capacity to confidently explore the world. Still, awareness of the other meaning of the cry, the potential for it to become "manipulative," keeps a competent parent on the tightrope even at this stage. Secure attachment? Yes. Slave to baby's command? No.

I can't stress enough how important it is to be responsive to a child's needs, especially in the first years. (A good rule of thumb for the tightrope-walking parent: early on, err on the side of availability and support; later on, err on the side of letting them manage.) If we must sometimes err on the side of "neglect," then we must also be sure that our child can handle it. We need to subject our kids to the right amount of struggling, at the right time. Expecting a child to soothe himself and put himself to sleep at 6 months is too early; however, failing to expect him to do so at 6 years is too late. Obviously there is a lot of gray in between. My resiliency curve is doomed to be only the most general of measures.

Many co-parents get into trouble when the two parties have different ideas about how much the child can handle on his own versus how much supervision and protection he requires. This is when splitting often occurs. As parents differ on how much responsibility should be left to the child, they will start to respond differently to children's Stories of Woe, and then the vicious cycle we have seen will kick in: one parent's overly soft approach makes the other parent's responses harsher, and then as that parent becomes more severe, the first gets even softer. And so on.

Ideally, parents have a common notion of what kids can handle when, which lets them sidestep splitting, keeps their child on a healthy resiliency growth curve, and protects against damaging emotional or instrumental neglect. So, can we locate some points on these curves? I think so. I offer these as exemplars, not as a system. But by locating various milestones at various ages, it gives parents a reference for the countless other decisions they need to make in between. Here are a few examples:

8 months
Parental level of activity: extremely high. Your child can sit up, so you don't need to hold her all the time. The only kind of neglect a parent would want to show at this stage is the most mild kind, such as letting a child struggle with a new toy, crawling or beginning to feed herself in the high chair. Still, such standing back is essential. The infant lives in a world that is safe and loving, where good things happen lots of the time—feeding, stimulation, mutual laughter—and when bad things happen (something hurts, hunger beckons) a parent is there to help and make it better. This is the foundation of a secure attachment to the parents. But bad things do sometimes happen, that's the point. Bad things an 8-month-old can handle include experiencing internal pains and external frustrations; when they do, this is the beginning of the child's lifelong relationship with reality. At this age, always err on the side of

attention and response; you may not be at 100 percent responsible, but you're still at 99 percent.

18 months

The Care and Feeding of Children by Dr. Richard Ferber teaches parents a method for getting a kid to fall asleep on her own: they put her to bed following a pleasant ritual, say goodnight and leave the room. When she cries, the parents wait a certain amount of time before re-entering the room, soothing her, re-settling her and leaving again; repeat as necessary. I don't recommended this emotional weaning before 18 months, when the child has developed the skills needed to manage this important step, but there's no doubt that some parents who don't do this at some point are asking for trouble later. In a surprising number of the cases I see, children are still in their parents' beds, in one case as late as age 8. By that point, the parents feel quite helpless to change the behavior. Of course, requiring a child to soothe herself and go to sleep is transferring considerable responsibility onto her little shoulders. And it is certainly familiarizing her with reality: her terrifying separateness from her parents. But as painful as it is, children must take this emotional step early in life in order to be independently strong enough to handle the tough realities that lie ahead.

5 years

What painful, non-catastrophic "failure" could we allow at this age? How about not supervising the management of Halloween candy? Many parents take kids younger than 4 out trick-or-treating, but leaving them with that huge haul of goodies, unsupervised, doesn't feel right. Fair enough. But around age 5, kids are probably in good shape to be left to their own devices. Then you can sit back and see what happens. (I know all the dentists are going to be furious at me for this one.) Not every kid wolfs it all down immediately as most parents expect. A natural instinct to conserve often appears. Young children will sometimes find pleasure sorting their candy, organizing it, counting it and savoring how much is left. Not always, but never if you're holding the loot strings. So it's time to shift the responsibility. The worst-case scenario is that he does wolf it all down. The stomachache afterward, and then having to enviously watch his sister continue to enjoy her carefully saved candy, will be their own teachers. You don't need to wag a little finger.

Another example: a 4- or 5-year-old child can handle his or her parents going out on a date night and being left alone with a sitter, even though many children may protest, even vehemently. Again, this is the kind of "scraped knee" they need to experience: the 4-year-old child who learns that he can keep his parents at home by protesting loud enough about the babysitter, has probably just taken a big step backward when it comes to developing emotional resiliency.

8 to 10 years

By age 10, you want your child to have his own relationship with school and achievement. That means leaving him in charge of his own homework. An interested, sympathetic attitude that sends a message of confidence is your best bet when it comes to helping your child develop a sense of academic responsibility. If he's really developing a "bad attitude"—ignoring homework, not handing things in—get in touch with the school so you can strengthen that alliance and sort out the roles. Make sure the people at the school hear your message of trust and appreciation in them. They should realize you want them to be active in your child's life, building a connection with him but also setting limits and laying out consequences as necessary.

12 to 14 years

Now is the time to start turning over responsibility regarding the choices your child makes out there in the world. Learning where his interests lie and finding ways to support his choices is the way to go. Sometimes these choices wouldn't be what you would have wanted or expected—not wanting to go back to the same summer camp, wanting to drop hockey and pick up basketball instead, getting into a new culture or music or fashion—so it may be hard for you. But supporting him will help him develop his own interests and it will put you right back on the park bench where your child always gets the most out of you.

16 to 18 years

By this time, you should have given over authority on matters related to sex and drugs. Your children already know your opinions so you probably don't have to lecture either. Ideally, you are a person they trust to talk to if there is a problem. So when they're barfing in the washroom at McDonald's, they know they can call you and your response will be to come and help. Without finger-wagging. Avoid being a gatekeeper because they may soon be living among unsupervised hordes of like-minded undergraduates. Better to give them a chance at practicing being an adult in your home. Be a respectful witness. Don't draw attention to the embarrassing bits; instead, reflect an attitude that shows that everybody does dumb things. Be sympathetic. Expect him to treat you with the respect he shows for everyone else in the world instead of the old defiant way of relating to a parent.

Parental Perspective = A Confident Child

In the end, it all comes down to maintaining perspective. All the dos and don'ts in the world aren't going to help you as a parent if you lose sight of your own powerful feelings. Perspective means being aware of your own anxiety and how it can blind you to the actual risks your child faces, how it can fire you up to act and react when it may not be in your child's best interests, and how acting on your worries ultimately makes things more stressful for your child.

And it means being aware of your over-identification with your children's efforts, like me when I sat in the stands of the hockey arena watching Sam's tryout when he was a little guy. Well, I was over-identifying with Sam as I sat in arena—the awareness came later. The trick is to be aware of it when it's happening. We care a lot about how our kids do; an awful lot. To the extent that it gets us sitting on a seat watching them, this is a good thing. But it's easy to go too far, to need your child to succeed in ways that cause you to lose perspective. As I did that day. It turned out that Green Jacket who stopped me in the basement of the arena all those years ago would be Sam's coach for the next four years. And what a coach. As my son finishes high school, I am thankful not only for what this man did for Sam's game, but also for the irreplaceable experience Sam had learning from—*and respecting*—such a worthy external authority.

If nothing else, our neurotic parenting culture has turned us into a group of over-reactors. We are quicker than ever to get upset, to freak out, to lecture, to get serious with our kids when things go wrong in the programs we've put them in and paid for, no refunds. But when parents fail to respond in a manner that supports their child's ability to manage painful failures in the world, they don't give kids the all-important message of resilience they correctly sent when the child was 4. This is the real inadvertent negative consequence of our parental hovering: we unwittingly tell our kids that the knocks of the world *are* quite terrible, that they should be avoided at all costs and that, when they do happen, there must be someone else to blame. And that's why anxiety (either a devotion to avoiding it or suffering under its unreasonable weight) is a growing problem among our children.

When the small boy climbing on the jungle gym gets to the top, he needs Mom to witness his accomplishment to make it real. When she sees him, it validates his experience, and helps shape his sense of himself, someone who can do things in the world. This parental function can be seen as "minding" because the ideas the mother has about her son, what is in her mind as she interacts with him, are what actually shape his understanding of himself. When a parent is able to correctly understand how a child is feeling about himself—say, proud for getting to the top of the play structure—and conveys this understanding to her child ("Look at you!"), this is when the child feels confirmed as worthy and capable. The child picks up this image of himself in the parent's mind—*this becomes how he sees himself*. And he needs his parents' validation for this to happen.

When he gets to the top and yells "Look, Mom!" the boy sees his parents' picture of him in a positive way: big and strong and great! But it works both ways. Parents' perceptions of their kid—the way they see him, the light in which they view him, both good and bad, affect the child. Constant worry about his ability to take care of things and to be okay doesn't give a child confidence; on the contrary, it stresses him out because he sees a picture of himself as somehow not properly equipped. He learns: "This *is* something to worry about." When parents see their child as someone who at any moment could lose ground in the rat race of life, they not only detract from his confidence, they also make reality seem like the looming conveyor belt of life. It doesn't matter what we *say* to our children when they start to succumb to this pressure; despite the "positives" we shower on them, the pep talks and anecdotes from our own lives, this anxious hovering speaks much louder than words.

Regular intervening also sets the bar *lower* than a child's actual capacities; it's based on an *underestimate* of what she can do for herself. And so, naturally, that's what she comes to understand about herself.

That's why staying calm, and keeping it all in perspective, is so important. Parents get this right when the child is 3 and running through the playground, but consider how different a message frantic parents send when they worry about marks and all the rest of it. We want to pull for their maturity. So I cringe when I see some of the regressive ways parents speak to their children, interactions that pull for their immaturity. For example, I hear moms (for some reason dads don't seem to do this as much) speak to their 8- or 9-year-old child in the third person: "Mommy's going to sit over here, okay, sweetie?" Consulting me because of their child's emotional immaturity, these parents are unaware of how powerfully the way they act and react deeply shapes their relationship with their children, and consequently the children's sense of themselves.

The good news is: many kids survive this over-parenting, and go on to adjust to the world and thrive in it. But some struggle well into their 20s. And perhaps beyond, who knows? The oldest failure to launch I have seen so far is a 29-year-old. I have yet to see any entitled kids come in as parents, but I know they'll be coming soon and I'm curious to see what kind of parents they'll be. Will the helicopter parents beget more chopper pilots? Or perhaps these kids will look back at how their folks raised them and say, "Well, that didn't work." If that's the case, the pendulum will swing back again—not all the way back to neglect, let's hope, but perhaps to the comfortable middle ground of benign neglect.

Doing Your Best

I consider myself a good parent, but I don't consider myself a great parent in the sense of knowing much about raising greatness. That's not to say the park bench approach doesn't lead to kids excelling at the highest levels—time and again, it does. But of course this approach is all about the child leading the way, so the parent isn't developing greatness in a kid anyway.

Certainly, we can all name a few infamous parents with famous kids. Think of the Williams sisters in tennis, or maybe the Jackson family's notorious father. Is this great parenting? I honestly don't know. What would these famous children tell us? I really wonder. But in a world where sports leagues give every player a trophy, it's essential to remember how important *not winning* is. Disappointing results are even helpful when you didn't do anything to cause the "failure." Just getting out there and striving is habit-forming, even when you don't get a gold star every time.

Perhaps the most painful disappointment my wife, Andrea, and I had to witness as parents was when our daughter, Claire, tried out for an AA hockey team at age 14. Wanting to make a team at the level below, she accepted an invitation to the tryouts for the top team in the organization (she knew the coaches for the A team would be there watching and picking the girls who didn't make the AA cut).

We were amazed at the skill level of the girls, and we were sure Claire was equally amazed to find herself in such company. And then we were truly stunned as we watched her play just like them. Suddenly, she was skating like the wind and playing defense like a champion. She made the first cut and the coach invited her to the next tryout, with a smaller group of candidates. Again, she made the cut. After the third and final tryout, the coach would cut three players and the rest would make the team. While Claire was quite anxious about this final tryout, she was pretty excited too, and wouldn't have missed it for the world. Prime conditions for flow.

The coach gathered the girls together at the start and the parents in the stands could hear him as he explained that three players would "cut themselves"—the three who didn't skate the final few meters of each drill, the three who didn't push themselves that extra little bit. It was a dramatic challenge. And the girls accepted it. After a fast-paced 45 minutes of skating, passing and shooting drills, the coach had the girls skate "suicides," grueling wind sprints, four players at a time. The last few meters are always torture, but these girls knew they could not falter. Again and again the coach blew his whistle; again and again the girls skated down the ice and back, down and back, down and back. And not one of them faltered. Not one. Even now, whenever I tell the story I can't help but tear up, but at the time I was weeping openly and I know I wasn't the only one. By the end, the girls were clearly in pain as they skated. But they didn't stop. No one was willing to cut herself.

When the whistle sounded, the coach skated to the center of the ice and faced the players, who were all doubled over or crumpled to the ice in utter exhaustion. He threw his gloves and stick to the ice, undid his helmet and flung it down, and then deliberately and slowly, he bowed to the girls, paying them "we're not worthy" homage. It's impossible to put into words the pride Andrea and I felt for our daughter at that moment.

That night, the wait for the coach's call was excruciating, but eventually, the phone rang and my daughter answered it.

"Yes, this is Claire."

A pause. "Okay, thank you," she said. "Yes, I understand. Thank you."

She hung up. We didn't have to ask. After a few platitudes and caresses, there was not much more to say as we sat there, the three of us, sniffling away on the couch. Eventually, Claire stood up. "Well," she said, "I'm going to bed." And we watched her slowly walk upstairs to her room.

We live in a society where parents sue hockey teams for such "emotional damage." And I can imagine some people reacting negatively to this story too. Some will question the coach's tactics and wonder if he pushed the girls too far in that final tryout. Or point out that, technically, he misled Claire since he'd told her she would make the team if she didn't cut herself, and, clearly, she hadn't. What kind of lesson is that about reality?

But that's all a bunch of baloney. It's true I had a bit of a tough sell the next morning when I had to wake up Claire for the A team's first tryout (she felt a little like quitting hockey at that point). But an hour later, the coaches signed her immediately and she was happy again. In fact, this experience taught Claire important things about herself, her strength and capacity for effort. In the long run it contributed to her willingness to "go for it" out there in the world. As painful as the experience was both on the ice (physical pain) and later on the phone (emotional pain), as a memory, the experience is an incredibly positive one for Claire. It is a memory of what she is capable of and a sense of what she has in her.

And for Andrea and me, this incredibly painful but non-catastrophic moment will always be an enduring testament to our daughter's strength of character.

Acknowledgments

This book is the result of more than 10 years of conversations with children and parents. Some of their stories appear in this book, although many do not. To all the families who have shared their thoughts and feelings with me, I wish to extend my deepest gratitude. Special thanks to those who have allowed me to tell their stories at greater length.

A number of teachers have shaped my thinking in important ways. Eli Sagan introduced me to the importance of understanding the history of childhood and the reciprocal relationship that exists among family, individual and society. Michael Schober supervised my dissertation and taught me, among many other valuable things, the importance of empirical observation and maintaining a healthy skepticism toward my own ideas. Over the years my clinical training has brought me into contact with many teachers and guides, too many to name, but those who have shaped my work the most include David Shapiro in New York and Roy Muir, Frances Newman and Art Caspary in Toronto.

Acknowledgments

A special thank you to Nancy Cohen and Diane Philipp, valued colleagues who provided helpful feedback on this manuscript.

To my friends Jim Risk, Steven Gottlieb and Lisa Kelner, thank you for being such playful and enduring fellow explorers in our often interweaving efforts to help children and families these many years.

I have drawn my material from many sources, but in the end it is impossible to escape the influence of my own parents, Peter and Sue Russell. Their wisdom forms the backbone of this book, while their love and support have made it possible in the first place. I am grateful to have the opportunity to thank them here for all they have given me.

Finally I wish to thank my own family—my wife, Andrea Lennox, for her love, friendship and unfailing support, and my children, Claire and Sam, for tolerating me as I struggled to write this book, for allowing me to share some of their stories and for always making it so easy to enjoy the show.

—Alex

Thanks to Trish Mercer, who read the first draft and offered such sage feedback. I'd also like to thank my mom and my sisters and their families (and point out that all their fears of starring in this book were unfounded). Finally, as always, special thanks to Carmen Merrifield. Writing this book may have taken less time and created less stress than the others, but your love and support were essential nonetheless.

—Tim

Acknowledgments

We'd both like to thank our agent, David Johnston, whose enthusiasm for this project and wise advice helped it come to fruition quickly and smoothly. We'd also like to thank everyone at Wiley, including Alison Maclean, Robert Hickey and especially Nicole Langlois, who asked such thoughtful questions and took such great care with our words.

Alex Russell and Tim Falconer
Toronto, December 2011